T0083644

BANGOR UNIVERSITY, 1884–2009

www.uwp.co.uk

British Library CIP Data
A catalogue record for this book is available from the British Library.

ISBN 978-0-7083-2226-0
e-ISBN 978-0-7083-2280-2

Printed by CPI Antony Rowe, Chippenham, Wiltshire

BANGOR UNIVERSITY
1884–2009

DAVID ROBERTS

UNIVERSITY OF WALES PRESS
CARDIFF
2009

To the students and staff
– past, present and future –
of Bangor University

Contents

List of Illustrations

1 Foundation Day – 18 October 1884 – at the Penrhyn Arms.
2 The first Senate, with Reichel in the centre (seated).
3 Sir Harry Reichel, Principal, 1884–1927.
4 W. Cadwaldr Davies, the first Registrar.
5 Earl of Powis, the first President.
6 William Rathbone, President, 1892–1900.
7 A student production of 'Twelfth Night' on St. David's Day, 1903.
8 Certain goings-on attract light-hearted banter in the press.
9 King Edward VII lays the foundation stone for the Main Building in July 1907.
10 The bilingual foundation stone – in Welsh and Latin.
11 The opening of the Main Building, 1911. Lord Kenyon opens proceedings, with King George V seated on the stage.
12 John Morris-Jones (left) and David Lloyd George outside Prichard-Jones Hall after the opening of the Main Building.
13 Kate Roberts, the distinguished Welsh writer, graduated in 1912.
14 The College's Officer Training Corps, being inspected by the Principal in 1912.
15 A Physics Laboratory.
16 The College rugby team in 1925/26.
17 Sir John Edward Lloyd, simultaneously Professor of History, Registrar and Honorary Librarian.
18 Sir Emrys Evans, Principal, 1927–1958.
19 F. W. Rogers Brambell on the marine zoology Easter course, 1933. Dates of terms were set in accordance with information on the tides – 'Brambell's tides' as they were known.
20 Sir Ifor Williams, Professor of Welsh and 'doyen of Celtic scholars'.
21 Wynn Wheldon, Registrar, 1920–33.

Abbreviations

AUT	Association of University Teachers
BUA	Bangor University Archives
DNB	*Dictionary of National Biography*
FRS	Fellow of the Royal Society
HEFCW	Higher Education Funding Council for Wales
MHT	Mountain Heritage Trust
NEWI	North East Wales Institute of Higher Education (renamed Glyndŵr University in 2009)
RAE	Research Assessment Exercise
UCCA	Universities Central Council on Admissions
UCNW	University College of North Wales
UCNW	J. Gwynn Williams, *The University College of North Wales: Foundations, 1884–1927* (Cardiff, 1985)
UCW	E. L. Ellis, *The University College of Wales, Aberystwyth, 1872–1972* (Cardiff, 1972)
UGC	University Grants Committee
UMCB	Undeb Myfyrwyr Colegau Bangor (Union of Students of Bangor Colleges)
WDA	Welsh Development Agency

Foreword

Prifysgol Bangor University has been at the intellectual centre of my life. At 17, in a spirit of inverted snobbery which has been a trait since, I refused to take my old grammar school headmaster's advice to apply to Jesus College, Oxford. Instead I worked to win a William James Lewis Scholarship to the University College of North Wales – as it was called then – in Bangor. In a move typical of the 'family University' which we still are even at 11,000 students, I was following in my father's footsteps.

He had been a star of Professor Ifor Williams's pioneering Welsh-language translations of Ibsen's modern dramas in the 1920s, as well as a tough and quick rugby half-back, a devotee of inter-varsity smokers, and a member of the Student Representative Council, before deserting the boards for the pulpit and becoming a divinity student with the Presbyterians. In much, but not all of that, I followed him.

It was in the Students' Union, on the stage of P-J (Neuadd Prichard-Jones) at would-be-revolutionary general meetings around 1968, or in the smoked-filled rooms of old Tanrallt, at inter-University debates, or heckling visiting politicians, that I learnt my politics. It was in Neuadd Reichel as a three-year pampered scholarship student that I learnt to be sociable, to drink sherry in the common room and robust wines with formal meals of fine Welsh meat. Ours was the first generation of male students to be allowed to entertain women in our own rooms within regulations on a sultry Sunday afternoon, between serious games of croquet on manicured Reichel lawns.

Moving from graduate to postgraduate in the hugely erudite School of Welsh, I was later to teach drama bilingually in the School of English, and to complete a Ph.D. in literary history and theory just before the regulations caught up with me. By then we were called University of Wales, Bangor, a form of naming which did nothing for us, I thought. A joyful moment tinged with sadness was when I succeeded my father's close friend and my boyhood hero Lord Cledwyn, wearing those amazing robes at graduation ceremonies in that same Neuadd P-J, where I had graduated, as President.

There are regrets too, not only the personal ones of loss of friends and colleagues over the years, but those of institutional failures. A particular period of estrangement for me was when Bangor became an arena of struggle for bilingual language rights to which the then authorities failed to respond in a positive way. I regret that I did not really try to improve my relationship with Principal Sir Charles Evans until it was too late. But that Wales now feels like another country!

My pleasure to have been a graduate, a postgraduate, a member of staff and finally President of my own University is second only to my unrelenting pride in our new-found independent University status and degree-awarding powers. Bangor is at once both the most Welsh in language and attitude of our universities, and the most international in aspiration and intellectual quality, serving its immediate community by raising its horizons of expectation. I hope that you will take pleasure in this splendid account of the institution's growth and development. We rejoice exuberantly in our 125-year family history as the old College of the North which, as Bangor University, still proudly flies the colours of the Prince Llywelyn!

The Rt. Hon. Lord Elis-Thomas, AM
President, Bangor University

Preface

Anniversary celebrations these days are 'ten a penny'. Some may seem absurdly trivial, others of profound significance. Several notable milestones are reached in 2009: it is eighty years since the 'Wall Street Crash', seventy years since the outbreak of the Second World War, and fifty years since the death of Buddy Holly. The foundation of a university may not bear comparison, in historical importance or public impact, with such events. Yet it will resonate, personally and deeply, with generations of students, staff and their families. This book is written to commemorate the 125th anniversary of the opening of Bangor University. It depicts a great educational institution, suitably conscious of its past, often unduly modest about its accomplishments and proudly and confidently facing the future.

I have not aimed to produce a comprehensive history of all the departments of the University. There will be many, I suspect, who will lament the absence of a particular subject development or departmental event, or the lack of reference to an individual. The book is, in essence, a general history of the University and a broad overview of its development. I have included what appear to me to be interesting and important episodes and developments. 'History', as A. J. P. Taylor once remarked 'is a version of events'. This is my version.

I should offer one stylistic explanation at the outset. In the interests of consistency, I have treated the names of all persons named, whether living or deceased, in the same way, by normally referring to their first name (or initials) and surname. Except in one or two specific instances, titles are not used.

I have many obligations to acknowledge. First and foremost, I should like to express my deepest appreciation to Professor Emeritus J. Gwynn Williams, whose magisterial book in 1985 on *The University College of North Wales. Foundations, 1884–1927* is a compelling starting point for anyone interested in the University's history and roots. Gwynn is, of course, not only a historian of the University, but also a former student and a senior member of staff during a critical period in its history. I have known him for thirty years, but the generous guidance and support he has given me during this project is far more than I could possibly have expected. Gwynn has read the whole of the book in draft form, and I have benefited greatly from his comments and advice. I am immensely grateful, too, to Professor Merfyn Jones, another distinguished Welsh historian as well as being Vice-Chancellor, for his encouragement and advice throughout.

I am deeply indebted to Einion Thomas, the University's Archivist, who has guided me expertly through the rich and fascinating University Archives. Einion has been unfailingly helpful at all stages of this project. I have also received assistance from Maxine Willett of the Mountain Heritage Trust, Nicholas Donaldson, the Assistant Archivist of the National Gallery, and Steven Wright of University College London Library Services, on specific issues. Mr Griff Jones kindly lent me material relating to his father E. H. Jones (Registrar during the 1930s), and Mr G. B. Owen, Professor Charles Stirling, and Professor Gareth Roberts gave me valuable documents. I am extremely grateful to Mrs Eleri Wynne Jones for very kindly granting me access to the papers of the late Professor Bedwyr Lewis Jones; and to Mr Dafydd Glyn Jones for drawing my attention to important personal documents which he had deposited in the Archives. Mr Alwyn Owens generously gave me his account of the career of W. E. Williams. Various other colleagues lent me books, papers or guided me to interesting material. I should like to thank Alan Parry, Elinor Elis-Williams, David J. Roberts, Wyn Thomas and Sarah Wale for assistance with illustrations.

I am greatly indebted to numerous former students and former members of staff who have sent me written accounts and reminiscences. In particular I should like to thank Mr Michael Barnett, Dr Gwyn Chambers, Ms Ann Clwyd MP, Dr Meredydd Evans, Dr Raymond Garlick, Dr Geraint Stanley Jones, Dr John Perkins, Ms Mair Barnes, Mr William G. Smith and Mr Andrew R. Thomas. Memories recorded by Dr Keith Ingold, Sir Dai Rees and Professor W. H. Whelan were kindly passed on to me by Sir John Meurig Thomas.

I have also benefited enormously from formal interviews or informal conversations with the following, who had first-hand knowledge of key developments and personalities in the story: Professor Colin Baker, Professor Tony Brown, Professor Juan Castilla, Lord Elis-Thomas AM, Professor Roy Evans, Professor John Farrar, Professor Ted Gardener, Professor W. Gareth Jones, Mr Griff Jones, Dr Geraint Stanley Jones, Mr Huw Elwyn Jones, Professor Fergus Lowe, Professor Densil Morgan, Ms Jan Morris, Mr G. B. Owen, Mr Alwyn Owens, Dr Dafydd Wyn Parry, Mr Jim Perrin, Dr Alwyn Roberts, Professor Gareth Roberts, Dr Gwyneth Roberts, Professor Ray Seed, Professor Eric Sunderland, Professor Charles Stirling, Professor Martin Taylor, Mr Dafydd ap Thomas, Professor Sir John Meurig Thomas, Professor Gwyn Thomas, Mr Gwyn R. Thomas, Ms Nans Wheldon, Professor J. Gwynn Williams, Professor Gareth Wyn-Jones. I am also grateful to Michelle Walker, a Ph.D. student in the School of History and Welsh History for transcripts of her interviews with several long-serving members of staff.

I must record my warm thanks to Dawi Griffiths who has diligently and skilfully translated the book into Welsh and to Sylvia Prys Jones who also read and commented on the Welsh version. This served only to increase my admiration for translators in general, and for the University's Translation Unit in particular. Sarah Lewis of the University of Wales Press has also been endlessly patient and helpful throughout.

For all secretarial and technical expertise – readily provided on top of her normal workload and the care of two young children – I am extremely grateful to my personal assistant Dawn-Marie Owen.

My final debt is to my wife, Dorreen, without whose unselfish support the book could not have been written.

David Roberts
Bangor

1

'North Wales and his wife will be there'
The Beginning, 1884–1892

'I consider the act of those quarrymen of Penrhyn. It is a noble thing for men sitting round this table to give their hundreds and their thousands; but for a poor man to give his £1 or his £5 out of his daily earnings means to deny himself something. That is real sacrifice.'[1]

A. J. Mundella's remark at the opening of the University College of North Wales in 1884 encapsulated both the romance and the struggle which characterized the University College's origins. Mundella, Vice-President of the Board of Education in Gladstone's government, made a stirring speech, frequently punctuated with applause, and 18 October 1884 was a day of jubilation in Bangor. A mighty campaign had triumphed. Yet the University College had had a difficult and contentious birth.

The drive for university education in Wales had always been inextricably bound up with campaigns for Welsh nationhood. Indeed, had Owain Glyndŵr's uprising triumphed in the early fifteenth century, his visionary plan for higher education – one university in north Wales and one in the south – might have seen a university established in Bangor before St Andrews (1412), Glasgow (1451) or Trinity College, Dublin (1591). As it was, higher education in Wales languished well behind Scotland and Ireland as well as England. Scotland had four universities by 1600 – over two centuries later Wales still had none. However, as national sentiment in Wales stirred in the mid-nineteenth century, so too a new movement to establish a Welsh university began to gain ground. Pamphlets appeared, papers were presented at conferences, and Welshmen, particularly in London, began to campaign. The University College of Wales in Aberystwyth emerged almost by accident in 1872 when the Castle Hotel in the town became available, but it laboured somewhat without government funding and was 'the Ishmael of Colleges' according to one observer.[2] Higher education remained pitifully inadequate as Wales entered the last quarter of the century.

Welsh members of parliament stepped up pressure, and in July 1879 a debate in the House of Commons on the subject drew a favourable intervention from Gladstone. A year later, when Gladstone was elected Prime Minister for the second time, he established a 'departmental committee' to investigate higher and intermediate education in Wales. It was chaired by Lord Aberdare, a former Liberal Home Secretary and, at that time, President of the Aberystwyth University College. Other members included Henry Richard MP (a Vice-President at Aberystwyth), Lewis Morris (Honorary Secretary at Aberystwyth) and John Rhŷs of Oxford (an Aberystwyth governor). The odds seemed strikingly in favour of bolstering the advance of the college at Aberystwyth. But it was not to be.

The Aberdare Report, which appeared in August 1881, was a hugely significant report for higher education in Wales. Its central theme was not unfamiliar: it recommended simply that there should be one university college in north Wales and one in south Wales. However, the report then made a momentous observation: the college at Aberystwyth 'whether retained on its present site or removed to Caernarvon [sic] or Bangor'[3] must be accepted as the north Wales college.

For Aberystwyth, those 12 words seemed to sound the death knell. They cast doubt on its continuation, and threw open other possibilities. Within months, a campaign in favour of Bangor had begun. In early 1883, a government grant of £4,000 per annum was promised to both the new colleges in Wales. Bitterness, wrangling and confusion lay ahead, however. The central question was the location of the college in north Wales, if it was not to be Aberystwyth. At a meeting at Lord Aberdare's London home, it was agreed to convene a conference on this matter at Chester in January 1883. Not surprisingly, Aberystwyth fought a valiant, eleventh-hour battle for survival at Chester, but influential north Walians closed ranks and outnumbered the Aberystwyth sympathizers. Harsh words were spoken and an amendment in favour of Aberystwyth fell – but, that aside, the Chester conference resolved little. A site committee was then appointed, comprising various official representatives of north Wales, and led by the Earl of Powis.

The site committee did not come up with the answer either, but in May 1883 they recommended that the issue be referred to three arbitrators: Lord Carlingford, A. J. Mundella (the government minister) and Lord Bramwell (a retired judge). This was a shrewd move, for the three commanded respect. They had already performed the same task in south Wales, choosing Cardiff in March 1883. The decision in the north, however, was to be somewhat more problematic. Whilst the north Walians at the Chester conference had been clear that they wanted a university college unambiguously in north Wales, they were not united as to the precise location. Caernarfon and Bangor may have been mentioned in the Aberdare Report, but other contenders appeared in 1883. Indeed, at the start of the arbitration process, 13 towns staked their claims to be the site of the university college in north Wales.

The arbitrators moved quickly to shortlist six towns – Bangor, Caernarfon, Conwy, Denbigh, Rhyl and Wrexham. Rhyl had assembled an intriguing case based, it seemed, on the climate there and 'a supply of free ozone'.[4] Denbigh had the radical Nonconformist editor, Thomas Gee (of Y *Faner*) in its corner. Wrexham was the largest town in north Wales, and was near to an industrial and coal-mining area, though it was also close to English urban and rural areas. Caernarfon, often considered at that time the capital of north Wales, had benefited from the expanding slate industry. Bangor, which exported slate from Port Penhryn, had been massively transformed by the advent of the railways in the mid-nineteenth century.

3

Houses and hotels had been built, and importantly, Coleg Normal, a college founded principally to train teachers, had existed there since 1858.

The vision that inspired the leaders of the movement for a university college in north Wales was matched by the grit and self-lessness of the quarrymen, farmers and others in the region who gave money (the so-called 'pennies of the poor') towards the cost of founding the institution. The Chester conference had resolved to raise funds for the north Wales college – wherever it was sited – and a number of prominent individuals present in Chester, including the Duke of Westminster and William Rathbone MP, pledged £1,000 each. The Penrhyn and Dinorwic quarrymen also took up the cause with enthusiasm, holding lunchtime meetings to pledge money. At one meeting, in April 1883, 42 quarrymen immediately promised £86 to the north Wales college: 'Dyna engraifft o'r teimlad sydd yn meddianu Chwarelwyr Bethesda ar y mater,' wrote the secretary of the quarry-men's committee. ('*This is an example of the extent of the feeling in the minds of the Bethesda Quarrymen*').[5] Many workers contributed a fixed sum out of their earnings, and ultimately the quarrymen raised over £1,250. Before the end of 1884, £37,000 had been raised in total from around 8,000 subscribers, and all but a tiny fraction gave less than £100. This is all now part of the great romantic story of the establishment of the university college in Bangor, and it should not be downplayed: there is no doubt that the idealism and strength of this local show of support helped to sway the arbitrators.

Nevertheless, there seemed almost as many arguments against Bangor as there were for. There were examples of poor health and social conditions (an outbreak of typhoid in 1882 did not help), and there were strong religious and political antagonisms in the city. That Bangor was held by many to be firmly Conservative and Anglican – through the influence of Lord Penrhyn and the presence of the cathedral – did not sit easily with some of the Liberal Nonconformist champions of university education in Wales. One writer to a news-paper recalled the poet Caledfryn's description of Bangor as a 'nest of bats and owls'.[6]

On 24 August 1883, the arbitrators announced their decision: Bangor was the selected site for the north Wales university college, and the decision was unanimous. They gave no reasons for this outcome and would accept no appeals. Joy was unconfined in Bangor. Last-minute protests from Aberystwyth were declared invalid, and some of the bitterness of the campaign remained for many years. Happily, of course, Aberystwyth also survived, helped by a government decision that it should receive the same grant as Bangor and Cardiff.

Establishing a university college is no trivial matter, and once the decision had been made the pace of activity quickened. A charter and constitution for the university college were drawn up and approved by the Privy Council in October 1883. Following Cardiff's lead, women were to be welcomed into full membership of the college and, significantly, the college was to be independent of any religious influence or control. Students would work for degrees of the University of London, as did students of many new university colleges in the nineteenth century.

The Earl of Powis, because of his position as president of the north Wales site committee took a leading role in the preparatory work, along with William Rathbone, the former Liverpool politician and businessman who had been elected MP for Caernarfonshire in 1880; the dean of Bangor and Thomas Gee were also active. Another important part was played by Henry Jones, then an outstanding young philosophy lecturer in Aberystwyth. Jones, the son of a Denbighshire shoemaker, had left school at the age of 12 to become an apprentice shoemaker himself. But after winning a scholarship to Coleg Normal in Bangor at the age of 18, he was to train as a teacher, become a Calvinistic Methodist minister and study philosophy at Glasgow. In 1882, to the fury of Aberystwyth, he became secretary of the north Wales site committee, and he clearly had input into the drafting of the political and religious aspects of the Charter.

There were few surprises in the election of the principal lay officers of the university college: the Earl of Powis became President, and the Vice-Presidents were George Osborne Morgan and Richard Davies, Liberal MPs for Denbighshire and Anglesey respectively. John Roberts, MP for Flint Boroughs, was Honorary Treasurer. In fact, for all the concern that the new college would be in thrall to Conservative opinion, to some extent almost the opposite was the case. Rathbone, fellow Liberal MP Stuart Rendel and Thomas Gee were all members of the University College Council. The first meeting of the Council took place on a Saturday, 8 March 1884, at the Queen's Head Café in Bangor: Colonel W. E. Sackville West, appointed to the Council by Oxford University, was elected Chairman, with Rathbone as Vice-Chairman.

The first university post to be filled was that of Registrar. W. Cadwaladr Davies, born and educated at elementary school in Bangor, had worked in the office of the *North Wales Chronicle* before becoming editor of *Cronicl Cymru*. A forceful advocate for higher education, he worked with the educationalist Hugh Owen in London in the 1870s, and after returning to Bangor in 1876 he played an active role in the administrative work for the new college and with the raising of funds. Intelligent and resourceful, his appointment was almost inevitable; he was later described as 'pre-eminently the man to help forward the new institution'.[7]

The appointment of the Principal, however, was a much different matter. The Principal was also to be the holder of one of six Chairs to be filled, and there were 21 applications for the post. The Council met on 14 May 1884, again at the Queen's Head Café, and interviewed six candidates. Three young men were regarded as particularly serious contenders: William Edwards, a native of Denbigh who had three Firsts from Oxford, a Fellowship from Jesus College and had been HM Inspector of Schools in Wales; Henry Jones, aged 32, already well known in Welsh educational circles and arguably the 'people's choice'; finally there was Harry Rudolf Reichel, the youngest of the three and the unlikeliest candidate. Born in Belfast, the son of the bishop of Meath and of German extraction, Reichel had pursued a brilliant academic career at Balliol College, Oxford, with four firsts and a Fellowship of All Souls by the age of 24. A glittering academic career undoubtedly lay ahead, possibly in Oxford. The appointment of a Welsh principal might have been expected in Bangor, perhaps considered inevitable. But there was no unanimity over the choice of a Welsh candidate. Each candidate was put to the vote, and with one dissentient – Thomas Gee – Harry Reichel was appointed the first Principal of the University College of North Wales at the age of 27.

In May 1884 the Council also appointed five professors. Reichel himself was to hold the Chairs of English and History. Henry Jones took his defeat with equanimity and became Professor of Logic, Philosophy and Political Economy. W. Rhys Roberts (Greek), George Ballard Mathews (Mathematics), Andrew Gray (Physics) and James Johnston Dobbie (Chemistry) were also appointed to Chairs. It was, without question, an exceptionally gifted group of scholars. Jones became an internationally renowned philosopher and was knighted. Ballard Mathews, Gray and Dobbie all became Fellows of the Royal Society. Curiously, there was no Welsh department or Chair: a dearth of candidates was essentially the problem. A Welsh and Classical lectureship was considered in 1884,[8] but the new College Senate could not recommend an appointment, and had to wait for John Morris-Jones's arrival from Oxford five years later. As well as the Chairs, lectureships in Latin, modern languages and Biology were established.

At first, it had seemed that there was no available building in Bangor to house the new university college. However, in April 1884, it transpired that the Penrhyn Arms Hotel could be leased from the Penrhyn Estate for around £200 per annum. Built as a coaching inn in the eighteenth century, overlooking the harbour, it had seen better days. Yet with some adaptation and renovation it was to be a valuable first home. The kitchen and scullery of the hotel became the library; science buildings were subsequently added and one of the stables became a 'smoking room'.

So on 18 October 1884, to an immense fanfare in the city, and with the motto 'Knowledge is Power' emblazoned over its entrance, the University College of North Wales opened. Flags appeared in windows, and an enormous procession – including several thousand quarrymen – to the University College building took place. The Royal Penrhyn Band marched, and local councils, schools, and various trades (printers, millers, bakers, for example) were all represented. It was 'one of the most brilliant spectacles ever witnessed in this part of the Principality',[9] and was followed by a lunch (at which Mundella and others spoke) and a concert in the evening. As one political observer correctly predicted months before 'North Wales and his wife will be there.'[10]

Once opened, with 58 students enrolled, there was no question of complacency setting in. The foundations were there to be built upon. J. J. Dobbie, a considerable scientist who delivered much-admired lectures, was instrumental in shaping the science programme in the

University College to meet the needs of the economy of north Wales. In particular, he played a leading role in founding in 1888, and securing a government grant for, an Agriculture Department, and an imaginative scheme for delivering agricultural classes in various north Wales towns. Dobbie also had a keen interest in geology, but another much-favoured project – a school of mining and quarrying – was never to be realized. In January 1889, John Morris-Jones was appointed as a lecturer in Welsh, establishing the subject in Bangor and beginning an illustrious career during which he was to exert a profound influence over Welsh cultural and literary life. In 1890, prompted by Andrew Gray, who had studied physics and applied electricity and worked with Lord Kelvin at Glasgow, an electrical engineering department within Physics was established. A lecture-ship was added, too, in zoology, and student numbers had by this time reached a hundred.

It was not all plain sailing, however. As the University College's first decade proceeded, there were demanding financial hurdles to surmount. The government grant of £4,000 remained unchanged, and additional funds had to be sought. But rural north and mid-Wales at this time was experiencing recession, and public donations began to dry up. In 1888, as a special Council committee was reviewing the financial position, Bangor's professors anticipated one of its recommendations by agreeing to accept reduced payments. This allowed staff other than the professors to receive some increase. The Council accepted the offer, commending the professors' 'public spirit and self-sacrifice'.[11] Some external help was also forthcoming. In 1890, Henry Tate generously donated £1,000 to a scholarship fund. Even more dramatically, in June of that year came news of the largest legacy the University College had so far received, from a Dr Evan Thomas of Manchester, and amounting eventually to £47,000. The 'Manchester bequest', as it became known, eased the financial difficulties and numerous developments (including that in electrical engineering) began to proceed.

Tensions – between Anglicans and Nonconformists, between Liberals and Tories, between Bangor and Aberystwyth – were never far from the surface in these early years. In 1889, the Council, led by Principal Reichel, objected to Aberystwyth's continuing use of the title 'The University College of Wales', and wrote to Aberystwyth on the matter, although nothing came of this.[12] Some of Bangor's leading figures were also changing. Henry Jones moved to pastures new at Glasgow in 1891. Ballard Mathews tendered his resignation, though he was persuaded to withdraw it. The University College's first indefatigable President, the Earl of Powis, died in 1891, and was succeeded by William Rathbone. In December that year, too, the Registrar, Cadwaladr Davies, resigned. He had encountered 'periods of stress and trial' in the post, and his health had been affected, but as the Council recorded he had been 'of the greatest possible service' to the new College.[13] In 1892, he was succeeded by John Edward Lloyd, who moved from Aberystwyth and became Registrar as well as lecturer in Welsh history.

Just as the challenges caused by these events were subsiding, the University College became engulfed in scandal. At its heart were various assertions by the head of the College's women's hostel (the 'Lady Principal' as she was known) regarding the conduct of a 26-year-old female student, Violet Osborn. Frances Hughes, the Lady Principal, had firm, strait-laced views regarding the behaviour of women students, and she ran an uncompromising regime in the hostel. During the late summer of 1892, she expressed concerns over Violet Osborn's conduct which were variously reported as accusations that the student was 'untruthful', was of 'an impure mind' and had engaged in 'indecorous behaviour towards men'.[14] Frances Hughes made a statement to this effect to the Board of Directors of the hostel – of which Principal Reichel and E. V. Arnold, Professor of Latin, were members. On 5 November, a small committee of the Board heard what was termed a 'rebutting statement' by Miss Osborn. Reichel and Arnold were convinced that the student's behaviour was not in question, and made a joint statement to this effect on 10 November. Frances Hughes did not agree. The Hostel Board decided to take no action.

The accusations, however, were regarded as extremely serious by supporters of Violet Osborn, some of whom were prominent in the community. On 10 November, two such individuals, Dr Griffith Evans, a well-known bacteriologist, and Henry Lewis, later Mayor of Bangor and a significant local figure, demanded a full investigation.

The Senate agreed, and a protracted and tangled enquiry took place between 14 and 29 November 1892. It quickly became uncomfortable for Reichel and E. V. Arnold, because as members of the Hostel Board they would need to be questioned as witnesses. Reichel vacated the chair of the Senate after five meetings, and Arnold also had to withdraw. Arnold had crossed swords before with Frances Hughes, and it transpired that at some stage he had offered Violet Osborn financial assistance with her studies. A third professor was then drawn into the web. E. Keri Evans, the young Professor of Philosophy who had succeeded Henry Jones the previous year, became implicated in the charges against Miss Osborn. After a reference was made to an incident, Evans was forced to subject himself to stern questioning by his remaining seven colleagues on the Senate. In his statement, Keri Evans recounted how on one occasion Violet Osborn had remained behind at the end of a lecture, and that as she was about to leave 'some papers which I had in my hand come into contact with her face'. Evans thought it 'absurdly trivial and – prudish imaginings apart – devoid of all meaning'.[15]

The Senate interviewed around a dozen witnesses, and considered many letters and statements. Violet Osborn herself gave a mature and articulate performance ('The whole affair has interfered with my studies,' she stated, 'and I cannot say whether I shall attend the Honours Examination . . .').[16] Various individuals gave powerful testimony on her behalf. The formidable Frances Hughes, however, declined to give evidence or to back up her charges. On 29 November, the Senate ended its enquiry with the judgement that there was 'no foundation whatever for any of the charges against Miss Osborn'.[17]

The matter was not laid to rest. It sparked agitation within the Council, not helped by the fact that the outcome of the Senate enquiry unfolded in the pages of the *North Wales Observer* before a report had been submitted to the Council – which raised the hackles of some members. Various motions and amendments were put, and eventually, in December 1892, a motion expressing satisfaction with the outcome of the Senate enquiry was passed by 13 votes to 8. Turmoil continued and a petition from eminent 'friends of Miss Osborn' asked the Council to 'neutralize' the effect of the charges against the student. The 'friends' included an MP, two Oxbridge professors, a vicar and a Congregational minister. In February 1893, the Council then passed another motion (by 13 votes to 9) asking Frances Hughes to withdraw the charges against Violet Osborn; failure to do so would lead to the removal of Miss Hughes's name from the register of lodging-house keepers.[19] It cannot have been a surprise to the Council that Frances Hughes refused to withdraw the charges, and the licence granted to the women's hostel was revoked. The Council took steps to reorganize residential arrangements for women, and a new 'Lady Superintendent' was appointed in 1893.

The reverberations from this crisis were felt far beyond Bangor. The press, in particular, had a field day. Frances Hughes sued the *Daily Dispatch* for libel following a scathing commentary on her supervision of the hostel, and she received £300 in damages. Her brother, the prominent Wesleyan minister Hugh Price Hughes, published some tart remarks in *The Times* about the 'unmarried young men' who ran the University College (seven of the 11 Professors were unmarried).[20] The matter was referred to in both Houses of Parliament, with Lloyd George intervening at one point. In October 1893, six members of the University College's Council resigned including the Chair, Vice-Chair and the Duke of Westminster, a Vice-President. Rathbone continued to work loyally within the Council, but his relations with Reichel were undoubtedly strained.

By modern standards, it was a storm in a teacup. But the University College was still in its infancy, and the affair unquestionably dented its reputation. The Frances Hughes libel case proved an embarrassment for Reichel and his colleagues with the judge and a barrister scoffing publicly at the learned professors. The local press felt it had all been a 'grievous blow' to the College.[21] It reflected certain attitudes to the education of women. There was a significant rift with aristocratic supporters of the College. It took a personal toll, too, on the leading players. The 'unmarried men' jibe may have hit home: at the end of 1893, Reichel announced his marriage to Charlotte Mary Pilkington, an old friend. He felt the strain of the difficult circumstances which had arisen, and in June 1894 he relinquished the Chair of English. All in all, the episode brought few triumphs. Frances Hughes lost her position, departed and married an Anglican clergyman. E. Keri Evans was perhaps the most harshly affected. Aged 32 at the time of the crisis, he had committed no great offence, and he was to secure damages and an apology following legal action against a newspaper. But it was no surprise that in 1895 he decided that his 'life-work lay elsewhere' and he resigned.[22] Although his health gave way, he later became a Congregational minister, was deeply moved by the religious revival of 1904, and became a biographer and gifted translator of hymns. E. V. Arnold, Professor of Latin, and a member of both the Senate and Council when the controversy erupted, also found that his life changed significantly: he married Violet Osborn.

During the tempestuous months of 1892 and 1893, the movement to create a federal university in Wales was reaching fruition. The idea had been gathering momentum, particularly following a conference in 1888 organized by the Cymmrodorion Society in London, which resolved to apply for a university charter. Bangor was the smallest of the new university colleges, but its representatives were prominent in the University of Wales campaign. Reichel himself was an active proponent of a federal organization, spurred on, doubtless, by his friendship with the Cardiff Principal Viriamu Jones. In Reichel's view, the University of London had been an 'academic midwife' to the Welsh colleges, but there comes a time when a midwife's work is complete.[23] In 1891 a charter committee was set up, with six representatives from Bangor taking part. Exactly one year later, Bangor's Council formally agreed that the petition for the charter be submitted. The charter application did not have a particularly smooth ride through Parliament, but eventually it received the royal assent in November 1893. Bangor, Aberystwyth and Cardiff united as founding colleges of the new federal University of Wales – a shining manifestation, it seemed, of Welsh nationhood.

1. Foundation Day, 18 October 1884, at the Penrhyn Arms

2. The first Senate, with Reichel in the centre (seated)

3. Sir Harry Reichel, Principal, 1884–1927

3. W. Cadwaladr Davies, the first Registrar

5. Earl of Powis, the first President

6. William Rathbone, President, 1892–1900

7. A student production of *Twelfth Night* on St David's Day, 1903

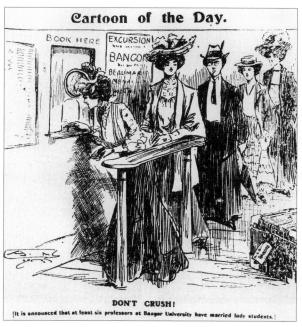

8. Certain goings-on attract light-hearted banter in the press

9. King Edward VII lays the foundation stone for the Main Building in July 1907

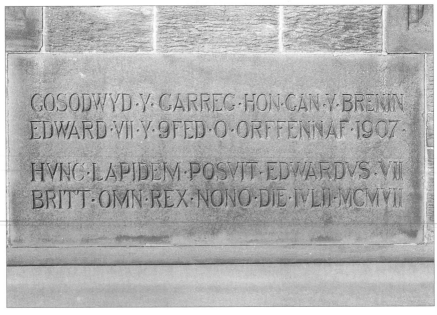

GOSODWYD·Y·GARREG·HON·GAN·Y·BRENIN
EDWARD·VII·Y·9FED·O·ORFFENNAF·1907·

HVNC·LAPIDEM·POSVIT·EDWARDVS·VII
BRITT·OMN·REX·NONO·DIE·IVLII·MCMVII

10. The bilingual foundation stone, in Welsh and Latin

11. The opening of the Main Building, 1911; Lord Kenyon opens
proceedings, with King George V seated on the stage

12. John Morris-Jones (left) and David Lloyd George outside Prichard-Jones
Hall after the opening of the Main Building

13. Kate Roberts, the distinguished Welsh writer, graduated in 1912

14. The College's Officer Training Corps, being inspected by the
Principal in 1912

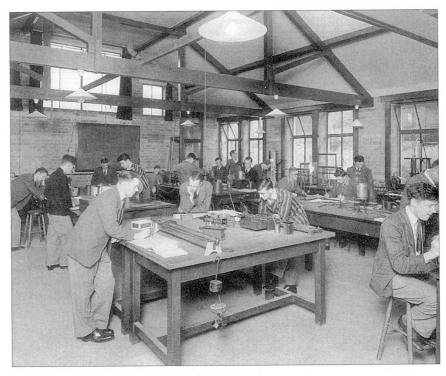

15. A physics laboratory

16. The College rugby team in 1925/6

17. Sir John Edward Lloyd, simultaneously Professor of History, Registrar and Honorary Librarian

2

'Little Balliol'
Growth and Development, 1893–1927

Despite trials and tribulations in its early years, the University College of North Wales had created a secure foundation. Around the turn of the century, more of its founding fathers – the first professors – began to move on. Gray, who became a Fellow of the Royal Society (FRS) in 1896, moved to Glasgow three years later to succeed his mentor, Lord Kelvin. Dobbie left in 1903 and was elected FRS the following year; he was knighted in 1915 for his service as Principal of the Government Laboratories. Ballard Mathews left for Cambridge in 1896, and he too became a Fellow of the Royal Society; he later returned to Bangor as an Acting Professor. W. Rhys Roberts, an outstanding scholar, moved to the Chair of Classics at Leeds in 1904.

Their successors were of similarly high calibre, and were unswervingly loyal to the Bangor cause. In Physics, one of Gray's own students, Edward Taylor Jones, a native of Denbigh, succeeded him in the Chair. Jones was to serve for 26 years before he then succeeded Gray again at Glasgow. Kennedy Orton, a St Leonards man who originally studied Medicine at Cambridge before turning to Chemistry and gaining a highly-acclaimed Ph.D. from Heidelberg, was to hold the Chair of Chemistry for 27 years. Orton had wide interests, his enthusiasms including music, rocks and birds. P. J. White was appointed to a new Chair in Zoology in 1895, and was in post for 34 years, developing an interest in marine science and at one time attempting to fund a Puffin Island biological station which had been acquired. R. W. Phillips, a product of Coleg Normal and Cambridge became Professor of Botany and occupied the Chair for 29 years. He was a leading scientist who contributed the article on 'Algae' in the eleventh edition of *The Encyclopaedia Britannica*. Thomas Winter, a Yorkshireman, became the first Professor of Agriculture in 1895, remaining in post for 18 years, and under him the department became regarded virtually as 'the agricultural headquarters of north Wales'.[1]

Thomas Hudson-Williams, born in Caernarfon and educated at Friars School, Bangor, had lectured in French and German before he took up the Chair of Greek in 1904 – a position he held until his retirement in 1940. Osbert Fynes-Clinton became Professor of French in 1904 (modern languages being divided to create departments of French and Romance Languages, and German and Teutonic Philology), holding the Chair until his retirement in 1937. A brilliant linguist, Fynes-Clinton studied the Arfon dialect of Welsh in his spare time and published a book on the subject in 1913.

One of the most versatile scholars was John Lloyd Williams of Llanrwst, who had been educated at Coleg Normal and became an Assistant Lecturer in Botany in 1897. But he also wrote operettas, and was a much sought-after conductor of choirs and musical adjudicator. His keenest interest was in Welsh folk-songs, and he played a leading role in developing music in Bangor. He moved to Aberystwyth as Professor of Botany in the First World War, and during his career received both a D.Sc. for his work on marine algae and an honorary D.Mus.

W. Lewis Jones replaced Reichel as Head of English Language and Literature. Another former Friars School pupil, he had worked as a journalist and contributed regularly to the *Manchester Guardian* after his appointment at Bangor. In 1899, Reichel also gave up the Chair of History, and John Edward Lloyd, the Registrar, became Professor of History for the next 31 years. Lloyd also continued as Registrar until 1920, and in later life would lampoon his role as that of 'lecturer in the morning, registrar in the afternoon and researcher in the evening'.[2] For a time he also served as Honorary Librarian (Thomas Shankland was Assistant Librarian). Born in Liverpool, but with family roots in Montgomeryshire, his *A History of Wales from the Earliest Times to the Edwardian Conquest* (2 vols, 1911) is regarded as a seminal work. He was elected a Fellow of the British Academy in 1930 and was knighted in 1934. Dignified, refined, always correct and formal – he was not one with whom people dared to be too familiar[3] – Lloyd was a truly renowned academic who must rank close to Reichel as one of the leaders responsible for the survival and development of the University College of North Wales.

At the age of 30, John Morris-Jones was elevated to a Chair in Welsh in 1894, the Council paying heed to the welcome growth in the numbers studying Welsh. He was one of Bangor's academic leaders with genuine star quality. A native of Anglesey, who had graduated in mathematics from Oxford but had read Celtic books and manu-scripts at the Bodleian Library, he was to become a poet as well as a major scholar and teacher at Bangor. His translations of 38 poems by Heine had considerable influence, though it was as a scholar of the Welsh language, and particularly Welsh grammar, that he is principally known. His major work, *A Welsh Grammar, Historical and Comparative*, appeared in 1911. In his early years in Bangor, he lectured through the medium of English, and his first lecture in 1889 attracted six College officers, two students and two strangers.[4] In some respects he seemed a disappointed man. Yet he was arguably the most inspiring Welsh scholar of his generation and was knighted (and acquired a hyphenated surname) in 1918.

The Chair of Pure and Applied Mathematics was filled for 30 years from 1896 by one of the most extraordinary academics to have served the University at Bangor: George Hartley Bryan. A formidable math-ematician, with a touch of genius, he was to make a striking con-tribution to modern-day knowledge of aircraft stability and aeroplane design. Bryan had analysed the theory of flight in an article in 1897, and in 1901 he lectured to the Royal Institution on the history and progress of aerial locomotion – a lecture which rather irked the great Alexander Graham Bell, then still basking in glory as the inventor of the telephone. When he heard of Bryan's lecture, Bell complained from Washington that he would now have to give up his own idea for a lecture on a similar subject.[5] Working with W. E. Williams, the son of a Penrhyn quarryman and a Bangor graduate in physics and mathematics in 1901, Bryan published the first results of experiments on the stability of gliders. Essentially what Bryan did was to apply the principles of mathematics to the question of aircraft stability. His book *Stability in Aviation* appeared in 1911 and led to the award of the second gold medal of the Royal Aeronautical Society, the first having gone to the Wright Brothers. The Fellowship of the Royal Society and other accolades followed.

Yet Bryan was also resolutely eccentric. His presence in the College was inclined to cause turbulence, and Reichel was said to have come to regard his appointment as a mistake. Bryan advocated the study of photography, railed against rules and regulations and argued that professors should not have to set and mark examination papers. It was said that on one occasion Bryan refused to attend a Senate meeting, but sat on the steps outside writing rude notes which a porter was instructed to take in.[6] The Council eventually received his resignation with equanimity in 1925.

W. E. Williams, however, went on to play a pioneering role in the University College. By 1910 he was contemplating building an aircraft, with financial support from H. R. Davies of Treborth, and a flight to collect scientific data was reported on in 1913.[7] Williams later became Head of an independent Department of Applied Electricity, and in 1942/3 became the first Professor of Electronic Engineering.

The University College's growth and development from the 1890s owed much to the intrinsic quality and dedication of its long-serving leading academics. But new plans were also hatched. The College opened a teacher-training department (the 'Day Training Department', as it was known) in 1894 to educate elementary school teachers. It was a conspicuous success, and the lecturer in charge, J. A. Green, became a professor in 1896. When he left for Sheffield in 1904, Green was replaced by R. L. Archer as Professor of Education. Archer, who built up the Education Department over the next 36 years, was one of the great characters in Bangor in the first third of the twentieth century. A father-figure to many (he was even known as 'Daddy Archer'), tales associated with his main passions – rugby and cats – abounded.[8]

Building on good work in agriculture, the College again blazed a trail in 1904 by establishing a Forestry Department, with the aid of a government grant. In agricultural education, it was believed that Bangor had 'set the fashion for the whole kingdom'.[9] Theology had specifically not been part of the academic programme originally, but the proximity of theological colleges and the recognition given them in the University of Wales charter led to the introduction of a Department of Semitic Languages in 1898.

A deep sense of indebtedness to the local community remained, and from its earliest days the University College had offered 'extension courses'. Much later, in 1910, a more systematic approach was adopted with the introduction of a 'tutorial class' at Blaenau Ffestiniog – the first such class in Wales. This 'extra-mural' activity was particularly associated with James Gibson, Professor of Philosophy, and later with R. Silyn Roberts, a former quarryman, Methodist minister and poet.[10]

By the turn of the century, the University College of North Wales was feeling buoyant, a national newspaper noting that it had grown with 'unflagging vigour'.[11] Student numbers had risen to 277 by 1900/1, and the Penrhyn Arms was no longer a suitable home. Five years previously the College Council had discussed with the Penrhyn estate the addition of some temporary buildings, but they were also considering the creation of a permanent university building. The issue was not unproblematic, and caused some heated debate: some on both the Court and the Council were not above calling for a complete relocation of the College. However, when the cooperation of the City Council was sought, it was forthcoming. In March 1902, the Corporation presented as a gift to the College a ten-acre site including the Penrallt land and part of 'Bishop's Park'. The College purchased a further five acres, and the location for a permanent University College building had at last materialized.[12]

An appeal for funds was again set in train. Rathbone, who relinquished the presidency in 1900 (and was succeeded by Lord Kenyon of Gredington), donated £1,000 to the building fund, setting an irresistible example which others followed. Between 1900 and 1910 a sum not far short of £100,000 was collected from friends, old students and local people. There were several villages around Bangor in which a donation from every household was made. In Llanuwchllyn in

Meirionnydd, which contained 163 houses, 186 people gave money.[13] There were other major supporters too. The Worshipful Company of Drapers give £15,000 to erect a library block, while the Duke of Westminster, the Marquis of Anglesey and businessman Owen Owen of Liverpool were among contributors. A significant development early in 1906 was the award of a grant of £20,000 from the Chancellor of the Exchequer.[14]

Henry T. Hare, designer of Westminster College, Cambridge among other buildings, was already a celebrated architect when he was selected in 1906 to create the new College building. He has rightly been lauded for his design. The building was to house the arts and administrative departments, the library, museum and a large central hall; there was room too for the physics, chemistry and other science departments at a later date. Interestingly, however, the central idea of adapting the building to the slope of the land, and creating a second smaller quadrangle, was not actually Hare's but that of Isambard Owen, then Vice-President of the College. But Hare enthusiastically revised his plans to take up the suggestion.[15] Hare's architectural style has defied some analysis. At an early stage, he appeared to be working in a late Jacobean style; he subsequently described it as 'late renaissance'. Some commentators have discerned Gothic characteristics, while others described it as 'Jacobethan'. What is clear is that Hare wished to associate the building in style with Oxbridge university buildings, but with due homage to Wales and Welsh history. There are seven statues on the exterior of the building – including those of St David and Owain Glyndŵr – and the arms of the Drapers' Company adorn the library wall. Hare gave the University College a building of which to be proud, at once dignified and noble, a 'majestical fabric' in the words of W. Lewis Jones, the Professor of English.[16] The head of an English University was reported to consider the building 'too good for mortal man',[17] while many more came to regard it as 'a lasting monument to the interest which the working men and women of Wales took in education'.[18]

The foundation stone of the new building was laid by King Edward VII on 9 July 1907 at an impressive ceremony during which a knighthood was conferred on Harry Reichel. In 1909, largely as a result of Lloyd George's persuasions, Sir John Prichard-Jones, an Anglesey man who had risen in the business world to become managing director of Dickens and Jones, offered to bear the cost of building the great hall. This was 'munificent liberality' in Lloyd George's view, and the University College Council warmly thanked both Lloyd George and Prichard-Jones.[19] In July 1911, a further royal visit saw King George V officially open the new building. In the end, there was insufficient funding to complete the main quadrangle, and the science departments remained in the old home for another 15 years.

As well as savouring the scholarly achievement of its academics, in its first 30 years the University College could point to some real student successes. A number of graduates – such as Ifor Williams, who graduated in Greek in 1905 and in Welsh a year later – were to remain and pursue distinguished academic careers in Bangor. Kate Roberts graduated in 1912, and was to become the leading Welsh fiction writer of her generation. Albert Evans-Jones (Cynan), who won the Crown at the National Eisteddford on three occasions, also graduated during this period. In 1916, Mary Sutherland became the first woman Forestry graduate in the world when she gained her degree from Bangor. She went on to work for the New Zealand Forest Service, who erected a plaque in her memory in woods in Rotorua.[20]

By this time, Reichel had served as Principal for over 25 years. He was not without his critics. The Violet Osborn affair led to his adopting a rigid approach to matters of student conduct. Some found his austere habits, such as his insistence on fresh air and open windows, somewhat alarming. He was also not a prominent public personality: a journalistic profile in 1904 pointed out that hardly anyone in Wales knew him.[21] In his personal dealings he could appear reticent – though one student later wrote that he had 'succeeded in breaking through that reserve' and found him a 'true "guide, philosopher and friend"'.[22] There was occasional sniping over the Welshness of the College, although Reichel actually made reasonably successful attempts to speak and write Welsh. The fact was, however, that Reichel was a man of integrity, who adhered strictly to what he regarded as the highest academic standards, and devoted himself unsparingly to the College. Yet, the strain of developing a University College was beginning to tell. He was taken ill in 1910 and was sent to Cannes to recuperate in 1911. Later that year his wife passed away.

The onset of the First World War inevitably compressed academic and student life. Student numbers fell away as many left to toil in the national interest, and some College rooms became military hospital wards. There were arguments at home as well as conflict abroad, and some conscientious objectors were present in the University College – even in Lloyd George's constituency. But in general there was widespread enthusiasm in Bangor for the war. In March 1915, 82 per cent of Bangor's male students belonged to the Officers' Training Corps, and Bangor had the highest percentage of servicemen killed of any of the Welsh university colleges. Former Bangor student Arthur Moore Lascelles, who was killed days before the Armistice, was the only person throughout the University of Wales who was awarded the Victoria Cross.[23]

It was during the First World War that the federal University of Wales had its first crisis of confidence. There were financial worries in all Welsh colleges, despite the fact that the government grant – which, astonishingly, had remained unchanged since 1883/4 – was doubled in 1909. In 1913, the McCormick Committee on University Funding paved the way for a more detailed reappraisal of the University of Wales. In addition, questions began to be raised over the efficiency of the federal system. Was there duplication? To what extent did the federal University coordinate the work of the colleges? Added to the mix was a proposal to create a national School of Medicine in Cardiff. The University of Wales seemed ripe for review. After much debate, a Royal Commission chaired by Lord Haldane was set up.

The Haldane Commission carried out its work in a febrile atmosphere. Relations between the Welsh university colleges veered from chumminess to suspicion, and back again, in short order. Both Aberystwyth and Bangor suspected Cardiff – not without reason – of separatist ambitions. Mary Rathbone, niece of the former Bangor President, felt that if Aberystwyth and Bangor teamed up they could be 'a real University for Wales'.[24] Yet Aberystwyth and Bangor had their own tussles. John Morris-Jones suspected in 1916 that Aberystwyth had hatched a plot to be the sole College teaching advanced Welsh. In fact, some in Aberystwyth were nurturing the vain hope that they could lure Morris-Jones from Bangor.[25] Thomas Jones, Assistant Cabinet Secretary, then drew up a plan for a more organized distribution of subjects across the Welsh colleges, but Bangor thought it heavily biased in favour of Aberystwyth.

So there was no shortage of apprehension, but when the Haldane Report appeared in 1918 most concerns melted away. The University of Wales survived, although the federal structures were to be substantially reformed. The university colleges were essentially left alone, and additional funding was called for. Lloyd George, the Prime Minister, was sympathetic, and it soon became clear that more Treasury funding, to match new local authority contributions, would be forthcoming.

The post-1918 period might have promised a return to normality, but in reality it was a testing time. Student numbers climbed spectacularly, from 135 in 1917/18 to around 500 two years later. The science departments were still in the Penrhyn Arms, and their accommodation needs were now acute. In 1917, following a gift of £20,000 from Sir Robert Thomas, an Anglesey man who had made his fortune in shipping, a North Wales Heroes' Memorial Council was formed to commemorate the north Walians who had lost their lives in the war. In particular, a memorial arch and new science buildings came under consideration. There was some delay, and considerable debate, before Henry Hare was selected as the architect in 1919, but he died two years later and was replaced by A. E. Munby.

Nevertheless, real progress was made. In 1920, the Memorial Council purchased City Mills in Dean Street to house the Applied Electricity Department, and in 1921 the go-ahead was given for the construction of 'inexpensive Science buildings'.[26] On 1 November 1923, with thousands of spectators present, the Prince of Wales (the future King Edward VIII) opened the Memorial Arch and laid the foundation stone of the new science buildings. Three years later, the science departments finally vacated the Penrhyn Arms.

Academic and administrative modifications were necessary after the war. In 1919, J. E. Lloyd, having been an unsuccessful candidate for the Principalship at Aberystwyth, relinquished the Registrarship at Bangor. He pointed out, with justification, that for 20 years the Council had had a Registrar and Head of History for the cost of a single salary.[27] Lloyd remained as Professor of History, and was replaced as Registrar by Wynn Wheldon. The son of a minister,

Wheldon had been educated at Friars School and the University College in Bangor (graduating in 1900) had then studied Law at Cambridge, and served with distinction in the First World War. He had been wounded in France and received the DSO in 1917. It was a fortunate appointment for the College, for Wheldon proved to be a skilled administrator and organizer.

In 1920, too, on the recommendation of Sir John Morris-Jones a second Chair in the Welsh Department, in Welsh Literature, was created. Ifor Williams, a Bangor graduate, was appointed. The Music department (though not formally recognized as a university department) opened in 1920, with E. T. Davies, the son of a Merthyr barber, as its Director. A year later a Department of Economics was founded, under the leadership of Robert Richards, later a member of parliament. In 1922, after adjustments to the charter to allow the teaching of theology, a Faculty of Theology was formed. Reichel was especially proud of this development and donated £450 to purchase theology books for the library. In the mid-1920s a scheme was approved for hydro-electric teaching in the Department of Applied Electricity.[28] All in all, substantial academic advance was recorded.

The tenor of student life after 1918 was utterly transformed. Before the war, although there were thriving student societies and sporting activities, the University College in general had the aura of a sedate, cloistered centre of scholarship – a kind of 'Little Balliol', as it was later depicted. Students generally were on a tight rein. There had been a mini-revolt in 1901 against the suspension of two male students who were found during the evening of a College eisteddfod 'whispering sweet nothings to young girl graduates'.[29] But such happenings were not common. After 1918, as hundreds of ex-servicemen enrolled, more boisterous spirits were to the fore. Some prim rules of conduct were relaxed, including that forbidding men and women from walking together in College grounds. Rag activities, a vibrant social scene, with more 'hops', societies and clubs, unfolded. Students were more inclined, too, to show their political colours. In 1921, a Welsh nationalist student society, y Gymdeithas Genedlaethol Gymreig was formed. By 1925, a new political party had been created in Wales, Plaid Genedlaethol Cymru, with ex-Bangor students Lewis Valentine and Moses Gruffydd playing prominent roles in its formation. A student branch at the University College quickly followed.

Principal Reichel seemed increasingly out of step with the post-war times. There were some who would have liked to see him retire at the end of the war; but it was quite usual in those days to work until the age of 70. In 1924, when Reichel was 68-years-old, the Council deliberated and invited him to continue in post until September 1927.[30] He was somewhat remote from normal College life, however, and he spent six months in New Zealand in 1925 as a member of a special university commission.

Of course, the bright young scholars who had set the place along its illustrious academic road in the 1880s and 1890s were now old men. Between 1922 and 1926, although no longer in Bangor, seven of the academic pioneers of the University College of North Wales, died: Sir Henry Jones, Ballard Mathews, W. Lewis Jones and J. A. Green in 1922; Dobbie died in 1924, Gray in 1925 and E. V. Arnold in 1926.

Reichel had presided over the establishment and growth of the University College for an astounding 43 years. A man of immense learning and devotion to the highest academic standards, his contribution to the University College of North Wales was inestimable. Reichel himself considered Rathbone the founder of the College; this has validity, but in truth it is difficult to see how Reichel's contribution could be surpassed. The title 'Rector Emeritus' was conferred on him when he retired in 1927, and he was elected a Vice-President of the College. Poignantly, Lord Kenyon, President since 1900, a major force in the creation of the new building and a close colleague, could not attend Reichel's last Council meeting in September 1927. He was too ill, and he died before the end of the year. An era had truly ended.

3

'The strange and beautiful hillside college at Bangor'
Recession and War, 1928–1945

The appointment of Reichel's successor in 1926 was by no means a smooth affair. The Council cast its net widely, and toyed with a substantial number of names. Four applications were received, and three were rejected as unsuitable; none of the three was Welsh. Wynn Wheldon (the Registrar), W. Garmon Jones (Professor of History at Liverpool and son-in-law of J. E. Lloyd), Ifor Williams and Ifor L. Evans of Cambridge (later Principal at Aberystwyth) were among the names put forward. However, a number of those suggested did not actually wish to be considered. The Selection Committee, chaired by Lord Kenyon and including Reichel, agonized most visibly over the candidature of Sir John Morris-Jones before deciding that, at 63, he was too old and that it would be a tragedy for Wales if he were diverted from his academic labours. After a somewhat arduous process of elimination, the Selection Committee opted for D. Emrys Evans, a 36-year-old Bangor graduate, and recommended him to the Council.

The Council was not inclined to acquiesce too readily in this process, however. On 15 December 1926, two Council members attempted to have the recommendation referred back, but they were defeated by 20 votes to five. The Council then voted to adopt the

Selection Committee's report by 23 votes to two. The matter appeared settled, and the Council adjourned for lunch. After lunch, Emrys Evans was summoned to make a statement to the Council and to answer questions. During the course of this, he ventured that 'if his appointment was likely to create any serious division in the Council, he would have to reconsider his position'.[1] When he withdrew, the Council again voted, this time on whether to consider any additional candidates: by a relatively slender majority – 17 votes to 12 – they determined not to do so. It was only then that the Council unanimously approved the appointment of the new Principal.

In fact, David Emrys Evans proved to be the man for the hour. The son of a Baptist minister from Clydach near Swansea, he had gained a First Class honours degree in Latin in Bangor in 1911, followed by Greek in 1912 and later an Oxford B.Litt. He had spent two years on the staff at Bangor before becoming Professor of Classics at Swansea. A tall, lean, scholarly man, he seemed well equipped to sustain Bangor's reputation and its adherence to high standards of learning and scholarship. By temperament he was reserved and cautious, declaring that he was not intending 'to make drastic changes'[2] – which was perhaps as well in view of the period of recession and war that was on the horizon. Emrys Evans was also determinedly Welsh, at a time when the Welsh character of the College was evolving. He was photographed with Saunders Lewis at a Plaid Genedlaethol Cymru summer school in the mid-1920s, although his interest in overtly political activities subsequently seemed to fade. In his first year as Principal, he submitted a paper to the Council averring that the study of Welsh language, history, literature and institutions was the primary duty of the University of Wales.[3]

With Reichel and Kenyon gone, the mood of transition from the old regime to the new was palpable. It was again felt acutely in the spring of 1929 when Sir John Morris-Jones died. The 'leader and inspirer of a literary renaissance',[4] Morris-Jones's academic record and reputation are unassailable, and they represented one of the cornerstones of the early development of the University College at Bangor. Four years after his death, a bust of him was unveiled in the College by Dame Margaret Lloyd George. There were other losses too. Philip White, Professor of Zoology since 1895 – and the first to suggest introducing marine biological studies – died in December 1929, and Kennedy Orton, Professor of Chemistry since 1903, passed away some weeks later. As a colleague remarked, the Chemistry Department was 'a family with Professor Orton as the father'.[5] During 1929/30 too, J. E. Lloyd, by this time a Fellow of the British Academy, retired as Professor of History. He had performed several roles heroically during his 38 years service, and his historical work certainly added significant lustre to the College. He remained active on the Council, and was knighted in 1934.

By 1930, economic depression had tightened its grip everywhere. Although its features differed from those in the south Wales coalfield, the combined impact of agricultural crisis, rural depopulation and falling slate prices provided a bleak backdrop in north Wales. Funding was scarce at the University College. The number of agricultural students had begun declining in the late 1920s, and in 1927/8 the Ministry of Agriculture cut its grant to the department at Bangor by 8 per cent. The department protested 'but without result'.[6] Bangor's student numbers generally seemed to decline compared with Aberystwyth, Cardiff and Swansea, and the proportional funding system in operation in Wales worked to Bangor's disadvantage. Financial limitations prevented a Chair in Welsh History being established in 1929, though an independent lectureship was created. In late 1929 senior professors protested about their low salaries, but to little effect. When the University of Wales Council asked all colleges in 1931 to consider economies in administration, Bangor sniffily agreed, pointing out that it had 'always been obliged to scrutinize every item of expenditure'.[7] The Library, too, led by former teacher Dr Thomas Richards ('Doc Tom' as he was popularly known) began to lose heart over its resources. Shelves and research rooms were full. Some staff, it was reported, were becoming ill as a result of increased pressures. The UGC was pressed to assist, but to no avail.[8]

All was not gloom, however. A new generation of scholars was beginning to make its mark. F. W. Rogers Brambell, a Dublin-born zoologist who combined a 'whimsical smile' with firmness of purpose,[9] was appointed Professor of Zoology in 1930 and began a long and distinguished career at Bangor. One of his early prescient actions was to launch a vacation course in Marine Zoology, initially at the request of King's College, London. Brambell's predecessor, Philip White, had interests in this area and had rented a pier kiosk from the Bangor Corporation as 'a small marine laboratory'.[10] But it was Brambell who was to drive forward ideas of developing marine biology. In due course, a Fellowship of the Royal Society and a CBE came his way.

G. W. Robinson, a Cambridge-educated scientist who had become Professor of Agricultural Chemistry in 1926, had concentrated his scientific interests on methods of soil investigation. His publication *Soils: Their Origin, Constitution and Classification* in 1932 was the first English textbook to be produced on the subject, while another, *Mother Earth*, in 1937 was equally influential. Robinson became the first Director of the National Soil Survey of England and Wales in 1939, and he too became a Fellow of the Royal Society and a CBE. J. L. Simonsen, who also arrived in 1930 as Professor of Chemistry, had already made a name for himself at the Indian Institute of Science in Bangalore. In fact, he was responsible for founding the Indian Science Congress Association, the chief Indian scientific organization. Simonsen was to stay in Bangor for 12 years, and he also received a Fellowship of the Royal Society in 1932, and was later knighted.

David Thoday, who had occupied the Chair of Botany since 1926, also carved out a formidable scientific career at Bangor. He had been Professor of Botany at the University of Cape Town before coming to Bangor, and he continued over the years to be a target for other universities. He was yet another in the distinguished line of scientists at Bangor who received a Fellowship of the Royal Society. (His son John, a graduate from his father's department at Bangor, became a renowned Professor of Genetics at Cambridge and a Fellow of the Royal Society.) In the field of Agricultural Botany, R. Alun Roberts was a leading light. A native of Dyffryn Nantlle and a cousin of the writer Kate Roberts, he earned a substantial reputation as a teacher and he published in his subject in Welsh. It was not until after the Second World War, after a period working for the Ministry of Agriculture, that Alun Roberts became the first Professor of Agricultural Botany. All in all he was to serve the University College of North Wales for 40 years, and he became the first chair of Nature Conservancy in the 1950s.

In the arts field, A. H. Dodd was another new appointment as Professor of History in 1930. The son of a Wrexham schoolmaster, and an Oxford graduate, Dodd was to establish a reputation for the highest standards of historical research. He wrote several books, including *The Industrial Revolution in Wales* (1933) and *Studies in Stuart Wales* (1952). He was also a firm advocate of his discipline, arguing crustily (but perhaps justifiably) on one occasion that the world would be better run 'if fewer of the people running it were under the illusion that history began in 1789 or 1815'.[11] He was a stalwart too of the extra-mural programme and of the Workers' Education Association (WEA), and he was to serve with distinction as Professor of History for 28 years. Welsh History had only a lecturer as its standard-bearer, but R. T. Jenkins, who was 49 when he joined the staff at Bangor in 1930, already had a major reputation as a historian and man of letters. His intellectual interests ranged widely, encompassing theology, architecture and French civilization, but it was his 1928 book *Hanes Cymru yn y Ddeunawfed Ganrif* (*History of Wales in the Eighteenth Century*) which won golden opinions. He eventually became a professor in 1945, three years before his retirement, and among many subsequent achievements was his editorship of the *Dictionary of Welsh Biography*. R. T. Jenkins was awarded the Gold Medal of the Honourable Society of Cymmrodorion in 1953, and became a CBE in 1956.

In the Welsh Department, Ifor Williams was amply displaying his fitness to follow in Sir John Morris-Jones's footsteps. Indeed, for sheer intellectual power and scholarship in Welsh literature, Ifor Williams's record can scarcely be bettered. Born in Tregarth near Bangor, the son of a quarryman, Williams had been bedridden with back injuries following an accident as a teenager. But he gained degrees in Greek and Welsh, joined the staff and was granted a personal Chair in Bangor at the age of 39, succeeding Morris-Jones in the established Chair of Welsh when the latter died. He published widely, but his principal field of research was the *Hengerdd* – the early Welsh poetry associated with Aneirin, Taliesin and Llywarch Hen. His most scintillating work, *Canu Aneirin*, was published in 1938. Ifor Williams became a Fellow of the British Academic that year, and was knighted in 1947. As a successor remarked, he was simply 'the doyen of Celtic scholars'.[12]

There were many other prominent scholars at Bangor in the 1930s. Harold Rowley (Semitic Languages) had previously served as a Baptist missionary in China, and won international acclaim for his Old

Testament studies. D. James Jones (Philosophy) was much admired by his students and published a study of Greek thought in 1939. J. Morgan Rees (Economics) was a leading authority on trusts in British industry. H. G. Wright, who served as a Professor of English for 35 years, brought the poetry of Edward Thomas to a wider audience.

At the administrative helm, too, there was fresh leadership in the 1930s. Wynn Wheldon had been considered a possible candidate for the Principalship in 1926, and was the subject of overtures from the Aberystwyth President in 1929 regarding the Registrarship there.[13] He was an able and efficient administrator and a move was perhaps inevitable. In 1933 Wheldon was appointed Permanent Secretary of the Welsh Department of the Board of Education. He continued to be active, and indeed influential, on the Council of the College, and was knighted in 1939. He would have been gratified that, many years later, a lecture was established in the University College in memory of his son, Sir Huw Wheldon, the former Director-General of the BBC.

Wheldon was succeeded in June 1933 by his neighbour, E. H. Jones. Elias Henry Jones had a wide-ranging and fascinating background. The son of Sir Henry Jones, and son-in-law of Dr Griffith Evans, his roots ran deep into the College's history. He was, however, born in Aberystwyth and had pursued a brilliant academic career at Glasgow, Oxford and Grenoble. After being called to the bar, he worked for the Indian Civil Service. He joined the Indian Army during the First World War, and was taken prisoner, held in captivity in Turkey and tortured. In the end, he escaped by feigning lunacy. In a best-selling book, *The Road to En-Dor*, he recounted his painful experiences, but subsequently he rarely spoke of them. After serving as secretary to Lord Curzon and the Government's Middle East committee (of which Winston Churchill was a member), he returned to Burma in 1920. He then retired early in 1924 to live in Bangor, and at the age of 50 became Registrar of the University College his father had campaigned to create.

By the time of the University College's jubilee celebrations in 1934, there were 636 students and around 94 academic members of staff. The jubilee was an opportunity to look back with pride on the College's achievements, but also to raise funds for further developments. A £20,000 appeal was launched, and the President, Lord Gladstone (who had replaced Lord Kenyon) set the ball rolling by donating £1,000 towards the Music department. The College made sure that its jubilee was appropriately marked (the Prince of Wales sent a message of support), but it was not a time to be extravagant. As the housemistress reported to the Jubilee Committee, 'a maximum of 500 to 600 teas is all the kitchen can undertake with a dignity suitable to the College'.[14]

Life in the 1930s may have had its grim features, but students at Bangor were neither downhearted nor inactive. There were many lively student societies. Some were associated with an academic discipline, such as Cymdeithas Llywarch Hen (for students of Welsh) or the Cercle Français; others were essentially discussion societies, such as the Wranglers' Club (which encouraged debate on any topic) and the Rockets' Club. Less official – and certainly less reverent – clubs also mushroomed. The XXX Club published a mildly mischievous magazine, *The Undertaker*, but steadfastly refused to divulge the editor's name, while the 'Q' Club fell foul of the University College authorities and was suspended for publishing derogatory verse about the Lady Warden, Muriel Davies.[15] There were forceful political societies, including the Socialist Club, the Radical Club and the Conservative Club (formed in 1939). The '20th Century' Club was created to promote greater prominence for women in College affairs, while the 'Gwerin' movement, founded by Goronwy Roberts, a patriotic Welsh student and a future Labour government minister, aimed to 'guard and strengthen the rights of Wales and of its people'.[16] The Anti-War Club was formed in 1935 as British government policy was shifting towards rearmament and reported 'a strong anti-militarist feeling' amongst students.[17] After the Armistice Day service in 1936, students processed through Bangor carrying a banner proclaiming 'Students Want Peace'.[18] The Student Christian Movement was also strong, students frequently helping to swell the congregation at Twr Gwyn Chapel in Upper Bangor. Nor did personal and social activities end with graduation. The Old Students' Association was energetic during the inter-war years, with dances, whist drives and 'charabanc trips' popular during their annual reunions.

The University was still relatively small, and had long developed something of a family atmosphere. In 1935/6, when there were 572 students, 90 per cent of them came from Wales. A noticeable number of students were the sons or daughters of Bangor graduates. Some, such as John Thoday and Daphne Robinson, were the children of professors. Moreover, a relatively high proportion of Bangor's graduates were to remain and find positions on the staff of the College. It was perhaps inevitable that this should occur in the field of Welsh language and literature: Ifor Williams, Thomas Parry and J. E. Caerwyn Williams were all alumni. But there were many other examples: Dafydd ap Thomas, who gained degrees in Hebrew and Latin by 1935 was to serve on the staff for 39 years; Hywel D. Lewis, was awarded an MA with distinction in 1934 and later joined the Philosophy Department; Huw Morris-Jones gained a First in philosophy in 1934 and was also appointed to the Department. Wynn Humphrey Davies, whose father had been an assistant to Emrys Evans, secured a First in applied electricity in 1933 and although he was on the staff for only a few years, it was the beginning of an association with the University College which stretched over eight decades.

Concerns for the Welsh language and for Welsh studies were to the fore in the 1930s. In 1934, the Welsh Studies Advisory Committee – in a paragraph apparently inserted by the Principal – reported that since the mid-1920s 'careful attention has been given to the question of Welsh qualifications in appointments'.[19] Amongst senior academic posts, Welshmen were reasonably prominent. Apart from the Principal and the Professor of Welsh, E. A. Owen (Physics), R. Alun Roberts (Agricultural Botany), Hudson-Williams (Greek), and D. James Jones (Philosophy) were among those who helped to give the University College an increasingly Welsh hue.

Students in the 1930s were also capable of rumbustuous behaviour. The College, as always, attempted to keep a firm hold on student conduct, though not with total success. Regulations in the 1930s barred students from entering licensed premises in Bangor unless they had the Principal's permission, while all students were 'expected ordinarily to be in their lodgings by 11 pm'.[20] In addition, in 1937 the Senate felt moved to ban the 'serenading of women students' unless the Lady Warden had given her prior consent.[21] At around the same time, the Librarian Thomas Richards – at his schoolmasterly best – was reporting disturbing behaviour: 'three gentlemen, two MAs and a trainer, tried to insert Dr Helsby's dog into the lower

Library; they were caught and will not see the inside of either library for the rest of this term'.[22] What most frequently ruffled the College authorities was the lack of restraint that appeared to characterize the annual Welsh Inter-College week activities. In 1938, the Principal in particular tried to halt the student Inter-College week, describing it as an 'annual plague'.[23] He did not succeed, but by this time graver events on an international scale were beginning to cast their shadow over university life.

Academic work was being seriously hampered as the decade wore on. Little by way of curriculum development seemed possible: ideas had not dried up, but the financial climate prevented the intro-duction of new courses. There had long been a wish to introduce Geology and Mining. In 1936, the Senate called formally for the establishment of a Chair in Geology, but the times were not propitious. There were proposals the following year to introduce Geography, but these too had to be sidestepped. Pleas to recognize a Music degree also went unheeded within the University of Wales. Towards the end of the decade, the Council decided to freeze the post of Professor of Greek following Hudson-Williams's retirement.

Meanwhile, established departments, particularly in science, were finding life difficult. Edwin Owen, Professor of Physics, complained about the urgent need for periodicals in 1935/6, while Brambell (Zoology) bemoaned the inadequacy of technical support in his laboratories.[24] There were structural problems too. A lecturer in agricultural chemistry in 1937 complained of 'grievous bodily in-convenience through the falling of water on his head' as a result of roof problems.[25] The Botany Department was regularly preoccupied with the presence of rats. 'Yesterday young rats had actually to be chased out of the laboratories. Miss Hitching reports that they are numerous' David Thoday recorded.[26] The fact was that the College's finances were decidedly shaky. As with other Welsh University colleges, Bangor's endowment funds were pitifully small. Student numbers began to fall from 1933/4, and income from tuition fees was 7 per cent lower in 1938 than it had been five years previously. Indeed in that year, the University College Council reluctantly agreed to increase fees by five pounds.[27] But by then, profound changes in the College's circumstances were in the offing.

There is no doubt that the University College in the far north-west of Wales, and particularly its imposing main building, held a symbolic, almost mystic, attraction for many – the 'strange and beautiful hillside college at Bangor' as C. S. Lewis, author of the popular 'Narnia' stories, depicted it when he gave a series of lectures there in 1941[28] (or 'y Coleg ar y Bryn' ('the College on the Hill') as it was often popularly known). It was also identified as a useful resource in the event of war. In 1938, secret negotiations took place at the behest of the National Gallery to house valuable works of art in Prichard-Jones Hall in the event of war. At the height of the Munich crisis in late September 1938, the urgent need for an arrangement became acute, and the College was warned to expect a consignment of works within days. Three days later, as Prime Minister Chamberlain returned from Germany to announce 'Peace in our time', came a telegram: 'despatch cancelled'. Of course the arrangement had to be resurrected the following year. A number of other buildings in the locality were viewed by National Gallery officials, and the Prichard-Jones Hall (along with Penrhyn Castle) made Bangor an 'admirable clearing-house as well as storage place'. In fact, fairly extensive alterations to the hall (including erecting steel bars on windows) were necessary to store paintings there. Over five hundred paintings – including some by Botticelli, Rubens and Rembrandt – were stored in P-J Hall from 1939 until 1941, when they were moved to Manod Quarry near Blaenau Ffestiniog. When war broke out, the director of the National Gallery, Sir Kenneth Clark, wrote to thank the University College of North Wales 'for the saving of so many precious pictures'.[29]

The most enduring impact during the war years came with the evacuation to Wales of students from the University of London. In November 1938, Principal Emrys Evans was asked by the Committee of Vice-Chancellors and Principals (CVCP) to consider how many such students Bangor could take. By the spring of 1939, it was clear that Bangor would be expected to accommodate most science students from University College, London (UCL). The uncertainties of the situation – with the loss of existing students if war broke out, but an influx of others from London – proved taxing for the Principal and the Registrar. In May 1939, Emrys Evans confessed to the Provost of UCL: 'I am not feeling altogether happy about the arrangements for accommodation under our scheme.'[30] The next day came a certain level of clarity: 154 UCL students would transfer to Bangor, and the College should prepare to receive a further 100 from the University of Liverpool.

In the event, no Liverpool students came, but 197 arrived from UCL. 17 members of the UCL teaching staff also moved to Bangor, including the zoologist G. P. Wells (son of H. G. Wells) and D. M. S. Watson, the distinguished palaeobiologist who had worked with Marie Stopes, had lectured at Yale and who was the first scientist to demonstrate that mammals evolved from reptiles. The eminent Elizabethan historian, John Neale, also came to lecture in Bangor. There was a minor rumpus over the financial arrangements with UCL – with the Bangor Treasurer Sir William Vincent admitting that 'our financial position is very bad just now'[31] – but eventually a formal agreement was concluded. The organizational hurdles were quite substantial ones. Many London students later recalled arriving at Bangor station at night in 1939, being allocated lodgings in Deiniol Road and being introduced to the more winsome procedures of Welsh landladies. ('If you want more bread and butter, please ring the bell,' one was reported to declare every evening after serving a meal.)[32] The UCL students used a bench in a room in the main building for their academic work until 1942 when a laboratory was set up in a former cycle-shop at 164 High Street.

All in all, however, the UCL arrangement worked. Unlike in Aberystwyth, where a degree of tension between local and London students manifested itself, UCL students quickly felt at home in Bangor. By October 1939, the Principal was able to advise his counterpart that 'things seem to be settling down here very comfortably'.[33] The secretary of the Senior Common Room, Dafydd ap Thomas, found his London colleagues 'a jolly lot'.[34] As it turned out, UCL buildings suffered more bomb damage than those of any other university during the war, and UCL staff and students were to remain in Bangor for five years. Some UCL students, such as John Hobart (Applied Zoology) were to stay even longer and became long-serving members of staff in Bangor. The end of the arrangement was widely viewed with 'unqualified regret', as A. H. Dodd put it.[35] When UCL staff departed, they presented their Bangor colleagues with bound volumes of the

Oxford English Dictionary in a bookcase made from wood salvaged from the damaged buildings at UCL.

The influx of London students enabled the University College to retain some semblance of academic normality. There were over 200 UCL students in Bangor for four successive years and, but for them, student numbers would have fallen to fewer than 350. As it was, the student population remained sizeable, and from 1939 to 1942 student numbers were at their highest ever level. This created headaches. Early in 1940/1, the Registrar was concerned that the dining hall was over-crowded. 'The room is apt to be full of smoke by 1.30,' he reported to the Principal.[36] Residential accommodation was not easy either. The Students' Lodging Houses Board, chaired by the Principal, struck 11 householders off the approved lodgings list because they refused to accommodate students, and many lived in cramped conditions. The Board was somewhat alarmed to receive a report on four households where students were 'sleeping together in double beds.[37] It necessitated immediate action.

The University College in Bangor may have been regarded by some as a safe outpost, but it was emphatically not sheltered from the impediments and restrictions of wartime life. Food rationing and a lack of consumer goods immediately had an impact. By the spring of 1940, many College buildings had been requisitioned by the government. An Air-Raid Precautions Committee was formed, and a warning siren was mounted on the tower of the main building. Up to 5,000 sandbags were ordered, along with picks, shovels, crowbars and two dozen hurricane lamps.[38] A 'nightwatchman' for science departments was appointed, and an air-raid shelter to accommodate 70 or 80 people was built on the science site. All doors except one were locked and bolted at 10 pm each night. Items of convenience, let alone luxury, could not be countenanced: in 1940, the erection of even a notice-board in the museum was deferred because of 'financial stringency'.[39]

The government took a robust line in demanding the use of College buildings. In November 1940, the suggestion that a machine-gun be placed on the College tower caused even Emrys Evans's usual courtesy and tact to wear thin. The designs of the armed forces were all too apparent, as the Registrar, E. H. Jones, recounted to a former colleague: 'You would not recognize the College today. The sandbags are in position, and the military in possession of a very large portion of the building . . . These are truly hectic times . . . The Golf Club clientele is becoming thinner and thinner.'[40]

Spirits were lifted in the 1940s by talented performers in the student community. The most celebrated of these, 'Triawd y Coleg' (the College Trio) – consisting of Robin Williams, Cledwyn Jones and Meredydd Evans – were hugely popular entertainers, and took part in some of the most influential Welsh radio programmes of the period. Staff and students persevered, despite difficulties. Senior academics lamented the fact that their students' education had been adversely affected by difficulties and shortages. H. G. Wright, Professor of English, found male students particularly affected by 'the atmosphere of general unrest'.[41] In Chemistry, too, J. L. Simonsen reported that his students were under 'not inconsiderable psychological strain'.[42]

The war years took their toll, too, on senior figures in the College. In the autumn of 1940, the son of the Registrar, E. H. Jones, was killed on active service. In December, E. H. Jones's health gave way, and he was given 12 months' leave of absence. Sadly, he never returned; he formally retired in 1942, and died a year later. He had been an adroit and industrious servant; and, given the prevailing conditions, a replacement was not deemed appropriate until the war ended. Sir William Vincent, who had been Treasurer since 1932, died in 1941, and for a period G. A. Humphreys, the Chair of Council, also fell ill. The Presidency had changed twice between 1935 and 1940. Lord Gladstone, son of the former Prime Minister, had been a devoted President, but he died in 1935 and was replaced by Lord Howard de Walden. Often unable to attend meetings, he resigned in 1940 and was replaced by Lord Harlech. The strains and stresses eventually told on the Principal too. In September 1945 he was given leave of absence to recover his health. It was acknowledged that his illness was the result of 'unsparing efforts on behalf of the College', and he remained absent for the whole academic year.[43]

Despite financial constraints and wartime restrictions on supplies, one significant building development was completed in 1941/2. Proposals to construct a new men's hostel, to 'assist in the social, intellectual and moral growth of male students',[44] had originally been put forward in the late 1930s. Principal Emrys Evans had visited halls of residence in other universities to view the most modern facilities, and in 1938 the Council approved the design for the building proposed by the well-known architect Percy Thomas of Cardiff. The costs turned out to be higher than anticipated but, with commendable determination, the College Council proceeded with the construction. In October 1939, the Council agreed unanimously that the hall should be named after the first Principal. Within three years, Neuadd Reichel had developed a remarkable community spirit, was being declared an unqualified success, and had attracted a large waiting-list.

By 1943, thoughts began to turn towards reconstruction. In fact, the Council set up a Post-War Reconstruction Committee in June 1942. Its first report in October 1943 was an ambitious but not unrealistic appraisal of the University College's needs and future objectives. The development of Marine Biology was recognized as a key priority for the future. The previous year, Rogers Brambell had put forward a far-sighted proposal to establish a Marine Biological Station in Bangor, and to acquire a 'seaworthy boat' for research. His vision was that the station would serve the whole of Wales and become a national facility. The availability of a suitable site and of ready supplies of sea water, as well as the required finances, were slight obstacles which would take some time to overcome. But an important step had been taken. In 1942/3, the Applied Electricity Department became the Sir T. D. Owen Department of Electrical Engineering, thus extending its academic scope. Forestry, too, anticipated growth and an opportunity to contribute to the government's post-war forestry policy. Geology had been contemplated on numerous occasions, and the Reconstruction Committee now considered it 'one of the most urgent new developments'.[45] The Arts Faculty pressed strongly to teach law as an ancillary subject, though the committee recognized the need to consider Bangor's relations with Aberystwyth in this regard. A new library and a Students' Union building were regarded as necessities.

The reports of the Reconstruction Committee provided important pointers for the future, and also helped to restore morale. By 1944/5, the burden and austerity of wartime life was beginning to give way to a new mood of optimism and aspiration. For students arriving in

Bangor as the war was moving to its end, the University College and its main building seemed to conjure up an aura of learning and sacrifice, but also of hope and confidence. As one such student, Raymond Garlick, recalled many years later, 'the great buildings seemed cold, echoing and half-empty when I went up to Bangor in September 1944'. He went on:

> In the windswept corridors one might still come across Sir Ifor Williams, the great scholar of the Gododdin, and Sir John Edward Lloyd, the Welsh historian. Outside the French lecture room Mlle Cariou, the *assistante*, was convulsed in tears over some new grief from France. In the Students' Union . . . ration-book appetites were assuaged with macaroni cheese, for most a new and exotic dish.[46]

18. Sir Emrys Evans, Principal,
1927–1958

19. F. W. Rogers Brambell on the
marine zoology Easter course, 1933

20. Sir Ifor Williams, Professor of
Welsh and 'doyen of Celtic
Scholars'

21. Wynn Wheldon, Registrar,
1920–1933

22. Students and sandbags on the terrace of the Main Building during the Second World War

23. An improvised Physics laboratory in 1942 in an old cycle shop

24. Valuable National Gallery paintings being unloaded at
Prichard-Jones Hall in 1939

25. The Main Building in the late 1930s

26. The 'Adult Training Orchestra', conducted by E. T. Davies,
the first Director of Music

27. Prime Minister Clement Attlee receives an honorary degree on the
stage of Prichard-Jones Hall in 1949

28. Westbury Mount in Menai Bridge, purchased as a home for the
Marine Biological Station in the 1950s

29. For many students, Prichard-Jones Hall was the venue for
College 'hops' (and examinations!)

30. Sir Willis Jackson, the eminent electrical engineer, and Principal Charles Evans at the opening of the Electronic Engineering building in 1959

31. The Students' Representative Council 1956/7; the President was R. Gerallt Jones, the writer and poet (second from right in front row)

32. The original dining hall, now divided into teaching rooms

4

'The whole place had a sort of family feeling'
Reconstruction, 1945–1957

When the war ended at last, bells rang out in Bangor cathedral and the University College buildings seemed, it was said, to blaze with light. An open-air service of thanksgiving was held in the College grounds the day after VE day. The treasures of the National Gallery had been removed, and Prichard-Jones Hall was put to use again for a ball and for graduation ceremonies. After recuperating from his illness, Principal Emrys Evans resumed his duties in the summer of 1946 in time to host a visit from King George VI and Queen Elizabeth on 18 July; they inspected the Library and P-J Hall. Some wartime images lingered. No sooner had Bangor bade farewell to UCL students than it welcomed a group of American GIs – still waiting to be posted home. In 1945/6, 75 American soldiers enrolled in the University College of North Wales; 25 Canadian servicemen were also expected, but did not actually arrive. A free place was also granted to a Czech refugee, Margita Marianna Barabas.[1] Some departments suddenly found their lecture theatres 'filled to overflowing' with American soliders.[2] Even more unsettling, they 'startled all by interrupting lectures by asking questions'.[3]

A fresh start was, however, being made. After a break of five years, the post of Registrar was filled – 'a first step in reconstruction', according to the Council.[4] The need to recondition, and in many ways rebuild, the academic infrastructure called for 'a Registrar of exceptional experience'.[5] In Glyn Roberts, the University College found one. Born in Bangor, and a history graduate from the College (having studied under J. E. Lloyd and A. H. Dodd), he had acquired both academic and administrative experience. He had lectured in History at Swansea until the outbreak of war when he had joined the civil service, rising to the post of deputy head of the British Raw Materials Mission to the USA. He was heartily welcomed when he took up his post in Bangor in October 1945, but he was to hold it relatively briefly.

Nor was it long before the University College had a new President and Chair of Council. The Marquis of Anglesey had taken over as President from Lord Harlech in 1945, but unfortunately he died within two years. For the second time the College once again turned to the Kenyon family. In 1947, at the age of 30, the fifth Baron Kenyon of Gredington, was appointed President. Bow-tied and aristocratic in manner, a prominent freemason based in Shropshire, Lord Kenyon did not seem an obvious choice for the University College as it entered the brave new post-war world. Yet his father had worked un-sparingly for the College, and the young Lord Kenyon's appointment was supported by both Welsh and non-Welsh members of the College Council. He was to serve the University for over 30 years.

A number of changes occurred amongst senior academic personnel. The Chemistry Department continued to attract scientists of an exceptionally high calibre. Simonsen had left in 1943, and had been replaced in the Chair by E. D. Hughes, a Bangor graduate aged 37 who was to become a chemist of considerable renown. A farmer's son from Llanystumdwy who developed a keen interest in greyhound racing, Ted Hughes was the first scientist in the UK to produce and use heavy hydrogen, and he was later to build apparatus to separate oxygen isotopes on a large scale. He was without doubt destined for an illustrious career, and he moved to UCL in 1948. To replace him, Bangor was able to recruit Stanley Peat, an organic chemist who had just received a Fellowship of the Royal Society. At Birmingham, Peat had worked in the research group assembled by Sir Norman Haworth, who won the Nobel Prize. Thomas Cowling, who was recruited to the Chair of Mathematics in 1945, was 'an astronomer by accident', to use his own description.[6] He was not the first or only mathematician at Bangor to have an interest in astronomy. G. H. Bryan's work also made an early contribution and, interestingly, the University College was presented with a six-inch refracting telescope in the 1920s as a gift from the sisters of the Revd A. E. Brisco Owen, and had an observatory overseen by the Physics Department. Cowling, however, was an applied mathematician who carried out pioneering research on the structure of stars, and he was elected a Fellow of the Royal Society in 1947, just as he moved to the University of Leeds. E. J. Roberts, a Bangor graduate and lecturer in agriculture prior to his secondment to the government's food production campaign during the war, returned in 1945 to the Chair of Agriculture. He was to spearhead research on livestock problems and lead the significant development of the College Farm.

In 1947, Sir Ifor Williams retired and was succeeded in the Chair of Welsh by an internal candidate, Thomas Parry. A quarryman's son from Carmel near Caernarfon, Parry was to make a singularly important contribution to Welsh literary and academic life with publications such as *Hanes Llenyddiaeth Gymraeg hyd 1900* ('A History of Welsh Literature to 1900') in 1945. Parry, in turn, moved to head the National Library in 1953, and was succeeded by another Bangor graduate and considerable scholar, J. E. Caerwyn Williams. Caerwyn Williams was one of four former students and members of staff – all in the Welsh Department – who became Fellows of the British Academy, the others being Ifor Williams, Thomas Parry and Geraint Gruffydd. A further important development after the war, with UGC financial backing, was the establishment of a post of Director of Extra-Mural Studies. Previously, established academics (such as A. H. Dodd) had overseen the organization of extra-mural classes on a part-time basis. In 1948, Alun Llywelyn-Williams, a poet and critic who had been taught at school in Cardiff by R. T. Jenkins, had graduated from Cardiff and had worked for the BBC before the war, was appointed as the first Director of Extra-Mural Studies at Bangor. He was to serve in this position for over 30 years. The contributions to the Welsh literary scene from staff who taught extra-mural classes are of considerable note. Even before 1945, R. Williams Parry, one of the greatest Welsh poets of the twentieth century, was a member of staff. 'Cynan', too, taught extra-mural classes for many years. Later Alun Llywellyn-Williams himself, and Dyfnallt Morgan were prominent figures.

As planned, the Chair of Greek was filled after the war by a distinguished classicist. R. E. Wycherley – a 'Shropshire lad', as he described himself[7] – had gained a double First at Cambridge, and had acquired valuable lecturing experience at Manchester. He was to occupy the Chair for 30 years, and his book *How the Greeks Built Cities* (1949) won immense praise on both sides of the Atlantic. In Philosophy, Hywel D. Lewis, who had carried out exceptionally original work in the field of philosophy of religion, succeeded D. James Jones as Professor. In October 1948, Glyn Roberts vacated the Registrar's seat for the new Chair of Welsh History, and was succeeded in his administrative role by Kenneth Lawrence.

In the five or six years after the end of the war, other new appointments were made of senior academics who were to dominate university life in Bangor for the next quarter of a century. M. L. Clarke (Latin), Dudley Littlewood (Mathematics) and Paul Richards (Botany) in 1948, Keith Spalding (German) in 1950, Ian Alexander (French) and W. Charles Evans (Biochemistry) in 1951, and Duncan Black (Economics) in 1952 were among those appointed to the most senior positions in their discipline. Black, who cooperated with the mathematician, R. A. Newing, gained recognition late in life, but he was a major figure. The Nobel Prize winner Ronald Coase named him alongside Adam Smith as one of six great economists. A number of younger academics, who were appointed to their first posts in these post-war years, were to rise to prominence during the 1960s and 1970s – including T. R. Miles, who was appointed as a lecturer in social psychology in the Philosophy Department in 1949, Gwyn Chambers in Mathematics in 1953/4, and Geraint Gruffydd (Welsh) and J. Gwynn Williams (Welsh history) in 1955.

The Reconstruction and Developments Committee had a sizeable shopping list of redevelopment work, including new appointments, the purchase of certain properties, new buildings for Forestry and Botany, a new women's hostel and an extension to the Chemistry Department. The development after which many in the College hankered – the establishment of a marine biological station – at last became a reality, though not without a final stumble. It was given the go-ahead in 1948/9, and the first Director of Marine Biology, Fabius Gross, was appointed in October 1949. However, he quickly became ill, and died by June 1950. A year later, Dennis Crisp, a Londoner who had been brought up by his grandparents (his grandfather was a crane driver) and who was a zoology graduate from Cambridge, was appointed Director. Crisp was to become one of the most influential marine scientists of the twentieth century. His paper in 1955 on the effect of water flow on the settlement of barnacle larvae gained him world-wide fame, and was being cited 50 years later. He was to build a department of international significance. Westbury Mount, close to the pier in Menai Bridge, was bought in 1952 and adapted with the help of a UGC grant, and it eventually opened as a Marine Biological Station in 1954.

Not all post-war ambitions were realized, however. For a short time, a head of steam built up in favour of establishing a medical school in Bangor. Local community organizations quickly lined up in support. The University of Wales appointed 'visitors' to examine the proposals, but they advised against the formation of pre-clinical departments in Bangor. The geology department, another favourite and long-standing idea, did not come about. In 1946, Emrys Evans thought it desirable but 'not practicable'.[8]

At the same time, heads of science departments fretted about the adequacy of their buildings and facilities. Raymond Andrew, Professor of Physics, in 1955 deplored the 'medieval conditions' under which they worked,[9] though he rejoiced that at last the department's 30-year-old typewriter had been replaced. Yet the record of the University College of North Wales for scientific research was steadily strengthening. The influential Brambell headed a vigorously active Zoology Department: at this time around 20 publications per year were being produced. Crisp and his Marine Biology colleagues were similarly productive. In Forestry, Eric Mobbs was developing research and teaching in colonial forestry, while Stanley Peat in Chemistry was fast establishing a reputation as one of the world's leading authorities on the subject of starch.

On the other hand, in the early 1950s the future of Electrical Engineering seemed – at least temporarily – less secure. The UGC appeared to form the view that an electrical engineering department without the presence of civil or mechanical engineering was not viable, and that in its place the Physics Department should simply offer an electronics degree. A critical point was reached in 1954 when W. E. Williams, the faithful Bangor servant and Professor of Electrical Engineering, moved elsewhere. Student numbers were low, and the department reverted to its old title, Applied Electricity. The situation was eventually retrieved, however. Emrys Evans appears successfully to have dragged his feet over the UGC suggestions, and in 1956 the College was fortunate to be able to appoint Malcolm Gavin, a resourceful leader, to the Chair. Very quickly, plans for a new Electronic Engineering building in Dean Street were set in motion.

Intellectual sparkle was added to the academic programme in the 1940s and 1950s by the procession of eminent scholars and public figures who made their way to Bangor to deliver guest lectures. The College's most memorable coup had been achieved in 1944 when T. S. Eliot, nearing the height of his fame as a poet, playwright and critic, gave two lectures in Powis Hall on Samuel Johnson – an event which attracted a large audience, including the vicar of Manafon and former Bangor student R. S. Thomas.[10] John Betjeman lectured in Bangor on Victorian architecture in 1952; Cecil Day-Lewis, collaborator of Auden and Spender, and later Poet Laureate, lectured in 1954; and Louis MacNeice, the Belfast-born poet, in 1955. Sir John Cockcroft, who won the Nobel Prize in 1951 for splitting the nucleus of an atom, visited the Physics Department and lectured there in 1958/9. The following year, Sir Isaiah Berlin lectured in Bangor. Unquestionably such visits were testimony to the growing academic standing of the University College.

There was precious little evidence of material prosperity in the 1950s, but students generally were cheery and energetic. Rag activities built up again, and there was something of a rebirth of political activity amongst students. In 1950, the president of the Debating Society, J. Gwynn Williams, was a member of a two-man debating tour of the USA. 'The English Debating Society was . . . a great training ground for some of us', recalled Ann Clwyd, a future member of parliament who entered the University College in 1956, and who remembers speaking in favour of a motion that 'Women should wear sacks'.[11] The English Dramatic Society attracted large numbers and offered productions ranging from Wilde's *Lady Windermere's Fan* to Aristophanes' *The Birds*. The Cymric Society for Welsh-speaking students was also enthusiastically active, and a bilingual student newspaper, *Forecast/Y Dyfodol* (later two separate newspapers), was regularly published. The Welsh Drama Society put on ambitious performances, including a memorable production of Eliot's *Murder in the Cathedral*, which starred Wilbert Lloyd Roberts – later director of Cwmni Theatr Cymru – as Thomas Becket. Sport took up Wednesday afternoons for many – and football matches between the University College and Coleg Normal teams were ruggedly competitive highlights of the year – but lectures would often take place on a Saturday morning until 11.00 am, after which a weekly sing-song would take place. For many students, the years at Bangor fundamentally influenced their lives in many ways. Geraint Stanley Jones, who hailed from south Wales and who went on to pursue a distinguished career in broadcasting, felt that had he not chosen to study at Bangor he would have lost his hold on the Welsh language.[12] Many met their future wives or husbands in Bangor; and many made lifelong friends from various parts of the world. '"Coll spirit"', a student magazine recorded in 1949, 'is far higher than in most' Universities,[13] and as one student who enrolled in 1951 later noted: 'the whole place had a sort of family feeling.'[14]

Important straws were in the wind in the 1950s with regard to the use of the Welsh language in higher education. A University of Wales Court committee had begun early in the decade to discuss Welsh as a medium of instruction in a range of subjects. At Bangor, Principal Emrys Evans chaired a committee on the topic in 1953. The Committee was favourably disposed to extending the use of Welsh, although the science representatives on the committee, perhaps not surprisingly, anticipated difficulties. Emrys Evans certainly prodded colleagues into looking seriously at Welsh-medium developments. 'The Principal thought it would be a tragedy if nothing could be done', the committee's report noted.[15] Three years later the University of Wales was urging colleges to 'appoint suitably qualified bilingual teachers',[16] and in 1957 it allocated £6,000 to appoint additional Welsh-medium staff. The first specifically Welsh medium appointments in

Bangor were in History and Biblical Studies. It was a small but significant step, 'an innovation in College History' as J. E. Caerwyn Williams saw it, 'and a change in the status accorded to the Welsh language'.[17]

Student numbers had climbed rapidly in the immediate aftermath of the war, from 380 in 1944/5 to 918 three years later. They remained high throughout the 1950s, exceeding 1,000 in 1957/8. Hard-pressed staff occasionally found the situation irksome: some scientists lacked the time for research ('the long vacations are not long enough', lamented Stanley Peat in Chemistry).[18] For others, even though there were structural developments for Botany, Forestry and Zoology, the buildings and facilities were sometimes found wanting. Even the Marine Biological Station seemed to have outgrown its Westbury Mount home by 1955/6, as the ever-exacting Dennis Crisp pointed out.[19] Yet it was clear by the mid–1950s that further enlargement was in the offing. In 1956/7, the College Council debated the implications of 'the large increase in student numbers expected in the next ten years'.[20] The impact of the 1944 Education Act was being felt in Bangor and elsewhere, and to the relief of university leaders, the UGC appeared able to rise to the challenge. In 1957/8, the UGC agreed to make financial provisions for new buildings in Bangor during the 1960–3 period: these were to include residential accommodation, a refectory, an animal house and extensions to the Physics, Chemistry and library buildings.[21]

As the first shoots of significant growth appeared, Emrys Evans's Principalship was drawing to a close. His stock could scarcely have been higher. His judgement, administrative ability and leadership skills were of an exceptionally high order, and much satisfaction was derived from the knighthood conferred on him in 1952. At that point the Council commissioned a portrait to be painted by Henry Lamb to commemorate his years as Principal. Few, if any, knew the stately Principal on a personal level. He 'kept himself remote', in the words of G. B. Owen, the Deputy Registrar at the time, claiming neither friends nor favourites. He was in fact a lonely man, but one who was regarded by everyone with the utmost respect.[22] In normal circumstances, the Principal would have retired in 1956, but the previous year the Council had unanimously invited him to remain in post until

August 1958. By then, he had led the University College for 31 years, and was 67-years-of-age. It had been a gruelling period, and only in his last few years had significant advance seemed feasible. In fact, Emrys Evans may not have found the spirit of expansion which was about to envelop the University College particularly alluring. He was ideally suited to the role conferred on him, and his achievement was that, despite constraints, he ensured that by the end of the 1950s the academic reputation of the College stood high. Like Reichel before him, he was given the title 'Rector Emeritus', and served as Vice-President for a period from 1961.

So, for only the third time in over 70 years, a committee was formed to appoint a Principal. Lord Kenyon took the Chair, and the outgoing Principal was a member – a curious aspect to a modern eye, though Sir Harry Reichel had also been on the committee which appointed his successor in 1926. Sir Wynn Wheldon, the former Registrar and a member of the Council, was an influential member of the appointing committee, as was Lady Artemus Jones. Rogers Brambell, now the academic elder statesman, represented the Senate, and Principal Anthony Steel of Cardiff was the external member.

There was no shortage of credible candidates. Idris Foster (Professor of Celtic at Oxford), Glyn Roberts (former Registrar and now Professor of Welsh History), and D. W. T. Jenkins (Professor of Education) were contenders. For many, Thomas Parry (former Professor of Welsh in Bangor and at that time National Librarian) was the favourite. Five candidates in all were invited to meet the appointing committee in London. The committee would have been acutely sensitive to the need to choose with care. In the spring of 1957, when it began its work, the Principal at Aberystwyth, Goronwy Rees, had been forced to resign in very public and controversial circumstances. Four of the candidates would have been very well known to the committee. However, it was to be the fifth candidate, a man with no professional academic experience, whom the committee recommended for appointment.

Robert Charles Evans was born to Welsh parents in Liverpool in 1918, a few months after his father had been killed in the First World War. He was brought up by his mother in Dyffryn Clwyd, speaking only Welsh until the age of six, but he then won a scholarship to Shrewsbury School, proceeding from there to University College,

Oxford, in 1939 to study medicine. After qualifying in 1943, he was called up into the Royal Army Medical Corps, was posted to India and Burma (where he learned Hindi) and was mentioned in dispatches. When he was demobilized in 1946, he moved to Liverpool to train as a neurosurgeon. He was appointed as surgical registrar at the Northern Hospital, Liverpool, in 1949 – the year in which he became a Fellow of the Royal College of Surgeons. Charles Evans's Welsh Nonconformist roots appeared strong. Thomas Charles, the nineteenth-century Welsh Methodist leader was one of his forefathers, as was Thomas Charles Edwards, the first Principal at Aberystwyth. Yet Evans's own credentials for the most senior academic position in the University College of North Wales were somewhat unconventional.

The central fact about Charles Evans was that he was a heroic figure in the 1950s, an adventurer in an era of triumphant mountaineering exploration. He had secured a place in history at the age of 35 as deputy leader of the celebrated team which conquered Everest in 1953. He was an experienced and respected climber when he was chosen for the role as deputy to Colonel John Hunt. He had grown to love the mountains of north Wales during his schooldays, had joined the Mountaineering Club at Oxford and had experienced his first Alpine season in 1939. Jan Morris, *The Times* reporter on the historic Everest expedition, found him 'a delightful trekking companion'. 'He loved the Himalayas and felt liberated there,' she recalled later.[23] In fact, Evans's fame might have been even greater. On 26 May 1953, having reached the South Col, he and another team member, Tom Bourdillon, were selected to make the first assault on the main summit. They did not succeed: faulty oxygen equipment prompted Evans to take the fateful decision to turn back. Three days later, Edmund Hillary and Tensing Norgay led a second assault and this time reached the summit of the world's highest mountain. Evans and Bourdillon had come within 300 feet of becoming the most acclaimed mountaineers in the world. The news of the conquest was broken to an excited world on the morning of the Queen's coronation, and the team returned to London to a heroes' welcome – all, that is, except Charles Evans, who, tellingly, made his way quietly to Nepal. 'There will be a lot of feting,' he admitted privately to a friend. 'I wouldn't mind a party myself but I'd rather be in the mountains.'[24]

The following year, Evans led the expedition which successfully climbed Kangchenjunga, the world's third highest peak and possibly, in strict mountaineering terms, a finer achievement than Everest. Evans published an elegant account of his campaign – *Kangchenjunga: The Untrodden Path* (he was also a skilled artist and drew a number of illustrations in the book) – in 1956, by which time he was a well-known lecturer on such topics. Along with Edmund Hillary, Jan Morris and other Everest colleagues, he embarked on a lecture tour of the USA in 1955 and was received by President Eisenhower at the White House. In 1957, Evans and Dennis Davies reached the summit of Annapurna 4, in what turned out to be his last expedition.

By this time, his considerable mountaineering activity was having an impact on his medical commitments, and in the mid-1950s he ceased to practise as a neurosurgeon, returning to general surgery. Precisely why he forsook medicine altogether for the Principalship of the University College in Bangor is unclear. Nor was the rationale of the appointing committee in selecting Charles Evans fully explained. It is likely that they considered that this all-action Welsh hero might appeal to the growing numbers of young people who were now looking for a university education and to those attracted by the mountains of Snowdonia. In any event, on 7 August 1957, the Council unanimously appointed Charles Evans as Principal from 1 September 1958.

Charles Evans had little time for the paraphernalia of fame and celebrity. Just before the Everest expedition, he privately revealed his philosophical view of individual success: 'I don't think it is so important,' he wrote to a friend '– though it would not do to broadcast that opinion. It would be possible, wouldn't it, for a man to stand on top and yet to have failed.'[25] Norman Hardie, a climbing colleague in 1954, said 'we all felt humbled by this man's quiet authority'[26] A longstanding medical friend from Liverpool regarded him as 'a born leader of men . . . quiet and introspective'.[27] The Council of the University College of North Wales had appointed as Principal a private and thoughtful man, who had no experience of academic life or university administration, but who had displayed qualities of leadership, bravery and determination. They were qualities which were to be powerfully tested during the next quarter of a century.

5

'Universities have a duty to try to find places for all those who wish to enter'

The Challenges of Expansion, 1958–1976

It is difficult to pinpoint precisely when the symptoms became widely apparent, but the earliest days of Charles Evans's Principalship were to bring him personal torment, which was to impinge on his period in office and indeed his life. In the late 1950s, at around the age of 40, he was diagnosed with multiple sclerosis. It is understood that Evans's wife, Denise Morin – a notable climber herself – became aware of the condition on their honeymoon.[1] Evans told the writer Jim Perrin many years later that a fractured skull sustained when assisting an injured climber on Tryfan in 1942 was contributing factor.[2] Charles Evans's longstanding medical friend Anne McCandless recounted that Evans also blamed the anoxia he suffered on his last Everest climb. However, in her private unpublished memoir she also stated that she 'noticed in 1948 that his hands were tremulous'.[3] Glyn Roberts, Bangor's Professor of Welsh History, worried similarly about the Principal's health more than ten years later, without knowing the true situation: sadly, Glyn Roberts himself died much too early in 1962. Whatever its origins, to a fit man who loved the mountains, to an adventurer who had scaled the highest peaks in the world, this was a tragically cruel blow. It halted his mountaineering and skiing activities, although with the assistance of his wife he was able to sail for a few years. Charles Evans was to serve as Bangor's Principal for 26 years, but within a few short years of taking up the post he often had to use a wheelchair.

The late 1950s and early 1960s, as growth set in, galvanized Bangor's academic community and generated much excitement. By the time the Robbins Report on higher education appeared in 1963 expansion was well under way in Bangor. Student numbers grew by over 40 per cent between 1955 and 1959, and in 1957/8 – Emrys Evans's last year as Principal – they topped 1,000 for the first time. There was a confident expectation that there would be 2,500 students by 1970 (an expectation which was realized). The most clamant need at this time was for more and better accommodation, with science departments in particular feeling handicapped. By 1958/9, the UGC signalled its approval of Bangor's growth plans. Funding was to be made available for a £4 million development programme from 1960 to 1963, on the understanding that the College would find 5 per cent of the cost. At a special Court meeting in July 1959, the President and the Principal jointly launched an appeal for £250,000, with Alun Llywelyn-Williams, the Extra-Mural Studies Director, as organizer of the appeal. The UGC's core grant to the College also rose, and as a result significant academic developments – particularly new posts – were set in train.[4]

Some key personnel changes coincided, more or less, with Emrys Evans's departure: A. H. Dodd retired in 1958, as did R. Alun Roberts in 1960 and E. J. Roberts in 1961. From 1962, however, a torrent of new appointments and structural changes caught the eye. In 1962/3, there were 38 new academic appointments. A further 35 new academics were appointed in 1963/4, 33 were appointed in 1964/5 and 47 in 1965/6. This was advance on a scale and at a pace never before seen in Bangor. In 1962, Bangor produced the first psychology graduate in Wales; the formation of the Psychology Department, under the head-ship of T. R. Miles, hitherto a lecturer in the Philosophy Department, took place a year later. A Department of Physical Oceanography was established in the same year under Jack Darbyshire, signalling the further evolution of marine science. New marine laboratories were opened in 1961/2, but more resource was needed: the research vessel *Nautilus*, purchased in 1948, was condemned as unseaworthy (the

Prince Madog eventually arrived in 1968), while Dennis Crisp kept up his tenacious crusade for more accommodation.

In October 1966, the Department of Social Theory and Institutions came into existence – created, like Psychology, on foundations laid in the Philosophy Department – under the leadership of Huw Morris-Jones, a 'popular and versatile teacher' who had been a member of staff in Philosophy since 1942.[5] A Linguistics Chair had been established, with F. R. Palmer as its first occupant in the early 1960s, while the study of Russian began – albeit in a modest way overseen by the German Department – at the same time. Pioneering work in developing drama as a subject of study was carried out by Emyr Humphreys, a novelist and short-story writer who had previously been a BBC drama producer before joining the University College. By the late 1960s, drama had become a sub-department of the English Department.

New buildings came thick and fast. Halls of residence were erected: Plas Gwyn (in 1963/4), Neuadd Rathbone (1964/5) and Neuadd Emrys Evans (1966). The 'Chemistry Tower' as it was often known, opened in 1965/6, enabling the department to vacate 'the venerable Orton building'.[6] Sir Willis Jackson had opened the new Electronic Engineering building in Dean Street in 1959 (the old mill there being demolished), and a further new building was added there in 1967, despite the intervention of a large crane which crashed into the existing building in 1965. An extension to the Library opened in 1963, and in June 1964 the College took delivery of an 'electronic digital computing machine' (an 'Elliott 803') and opened a computing laboratory.[7] At the end of the decade, a new Students' Union building on Deiniol Road was constructed (in 1968), along with the 'New Arts Building' (1969) – completing the main quadrangle originally envisaged by Hare, but perhaps without his eye for nobility and tradition. In many respects these were heady days, and on the whole funding was not a significant worry. In 1968/9, Charles Evans was knighted for his services to mountaineering and elected president of the Alpine Club.

Scientific research burgeoned in the post-war period. The substantial number of publications recorded in *Annual Reports* from the mid-1950s attest to the growing volume and quality of the scientific work taking place in Bangor. Raymond Andrew, who became Professor

of Physics in 1954, carried out pioneering work on magnetic resonance. It was during his ten years at Bangor that he made the hugely
significant discovery of 'the magic-angle-spinning NMR technique',
now used in universities throughout the world.[8] There was research
too in the field of NMR (nuclear magnetic resonance) imaging, which
has influenced work in hospitals today. Andrew influenced a number
of scientists in Bangor, including the young chemist John Meurig
Thomas (later Sir John, Master of Peterhouse, Cambridge) who was
interested in the properties of solids. Thomas derived great value from
contacts with young researchers in Physics in Bangor, such as Gareth
Roberts (later Master of Wolfson College, Oxford) and Robin Williams
(later Vice-Chancellor of Swansea University) as well as with Robert
Cahn, Professor of Materials Science – the first such Chair anywhere
in the UK – in the Electronic Engineering Department. Robin Williams
started a collaboration with John Meurig Thomas and his promising
Ph.D. student, J. O. Williams (later Principal of NEWI). John Meurig
Thomas was, in fact, a rising star in science: he won the Corday
Morgan Prize of the Chemical Society in 1967, and was the first
recipient of the Pettinos Award of the American Carbon Society in
1969, the year he moved to a Chair in Aberystwyth.

In the biological sciences, John Harper – an Oxford-educated
agricultural botanist and a noted humanist – had succeeded R. Alun
Roberts in the Chair of Agricultural Botany in 1960, and was establishing an international reputation in plant population biology, a
subject he practically invented. He was elected a Fellow of the Royal
Society in 1978, and was appointed CBE after his retirement from
Bangor in the early 1980s. Harper single-mindedly focused on research
in his department – where other notable scientists such as Peter Greig-
Smith also built solid reputations – and in 1966 became head of a
new School of Plant Biology (a merger of Botany and Agricultural
Botany). The realignment put Bangor, he believed, 'a step ahead of
universities such as Nottingham, Reading and Oxford'.[9] Paul Richards,
Professor of Botany since 1949, was another Bangor scientist of real
international standing. A slight, scholarly man, he travelled widely,
taking part in many African expeditions, and was a leading authority
on rain forests. (His 1952 book *The Tropical Rain Forest* was a
classic text on the subject.) Later he was a member of the committee

set up by the National Science Foundation to investigate the use of herbicides in the Vietnam war. In the 1960s, Rogers Brambell in Zoology remained Bangor's most influential scientist. He won the Royal Society Royal Medal, awarded by the Queen, in 1964, and he retired in 1969 after an astonishing 39 years in the Lloyd Roberts Chair of Zoology.

Across the water in Menai Bridge, Dennis Crisp was leading marine biology from strength to strength. His staff recorded 46 publications in 1965/6 – far more than any other department. Crisp's personal reputation was also soaring. Juan Carlos Castilla from Chile, later an internationally renowned professor of marine ecology, was one of many who travelled across the world to pursue postgraduate study in Bangor in the 1960s solely because of Dennis Crisp's reputation. Crisp was, Castilla later judged, one of the three or four top marine scientists in the world at that time.[10] In 1968, Dennis Crisp was rewarded with a Fellowship of the Royal Society. Not everyone found him the warmest of colleagues: he could irritate as well as inspire, and he kept up, with great pride, a constant fight against, in his view, College bureaucrats and red tape. Yet in 15 years he effectively built Bangor's worldwide reputation in marine science.

The electronic engineers, spearheaded by Malcolm Gavin, were branching out, countering vigorously the view that they could not exist without mechanical and civil engineering departments. Effectively Gavin created new sub-departments of control engineering and materials technology – each headed by Professors Bob Paul and R. W. Cahn. It was, he argued, an 'experiment in university technological education'.[11]

In biochemistry, W. Charles Evans was also blazing a trail with his research into the biodegrability of various substances present in the environment. Evans, an engaging local Bangor man, and a gifted scientist who had worked in Sir Alexander Fleming's laboratory at St Mary's Hospital Medical School in 1944/5, was 'intrigued and tantalized' by the problems of bracken-poisoning in cattle.[12] Yet it was his work in microbial degradation which was to establish his reputation and form the basis of much present-day knowledge in the field of environmental pollution. He became a Fellow of the Royal Society in 1979.

The Faculty of Arts, too, could boast star academics in the 1960s. C. L. Mowat, who succeeded A. H. Dodd as Professor of History in 1958, had risen to prominence whilst working at the University of Chicago with an influential book, *Britain Between the Wars*, in 1955, and was unquestionably a historian of the front rank. In the Welsh History Department, J. Gwynn Williams became the third holder of the Chair. In his early days in the Chair, he followed in the footsteps of A. H. Dodd, a peerless authority on seventeenth-century Wales, but in response to pressing invitations, he subsequently devoted much energy to acclaimed histories of the early years of the University College and of the University of Wales. John Danby, Professor of English, was a charismatic teacher and one of the College's prominent characters. A short 'roly-poly figure of a man',[13] Danby was a leading Shakespearian scholar whose book on *King Lear* had apparently been published by Faber & Faber after he had been interviewed by its director T. S. Eliot. His lectures, too, were brilliantly stimulating. Yet Danby could be equally at home playing dominoes in the 'Ship Launch' by Bangor's pier.

Keith Spalding, Professor of German and an increasingly influential member of the Senate, had led an even more dramatic life. Born Karl Heinz Spalt in Frankfurt in 1913, he had become a pacifist as a teenager. At the age of 18 he wrote an anti-war book which had the distinction of being burned by opponents in front of Berlin University. When Hitler came to power in Germany in 1933, Spalt fled to Vienna, continued travelling and eventually reached Britain in 1934 where he began studying at Birmingham University. When war broke out in 1939 he found himself interned in Britain. After being released in October 1940, he joined the British army and played a part in the defeat of his home country.[14] He had joined Bangor in 1950 and was to stay until retirement over 30 years later. Spalding's services to lexicography were recognized when the West German Ambassador travelled to Bangor to pay tribute to him.

J. E. Caerwyn Williams, who left the Welsh Department for the Chair of Irish at Aberystwyth, was replaced by Melville Richards, then head of Celtic at Liverpool University. A Swansea graduate, Richards had been appointed to his Alma Mater in 1936, and was widely – and wrongly – thought to have filled Saunders Lewis's post after the latter's dismissal following his involvement in the burning of the Pen-y-berth bombing school. Melville Richards's published work included handbooks of Old Irish and modern Welsh syntax, but he gained widest recognition for his work on Welsh place-name studies. Indeed, the Melville Richards Archive in the University is a veritable treasure-house for students of Welsh place names.

In Music, D. E. Parry Williams – who had originally studied science – was moulding a substantial department which attracted some fine young academics and musicians. Reginald Smith-Brindle's compositions were being performed throughout Europe, while Bernard Rands, an Englishman who came to Bangor to study and learnt Welsh, was similarly prolific. Rands was later to make his name in the USA as a first-rate composer and Professor of Music at Harvard, and was to win a Pulitzer Prize. William Mathias, a product of Carmarthenshire who had started playing the piano at the age of three and composing at the age of five, was another outstanding young composer in the department. He became a Fellow of the Royal Academy of Music in 1965 at the age of 31.

Clement Mundle and Ian Alexander were two prominent Scots on the Senate. Mundle, an authority on psychical research and clairvoyance, had succeeded Hywel D. Lewis in 1955 and was the latest in a long line of distinguished Philosophy professors. Alexander had emphasized the study of French existential philosophy during his tenure of the Chair of French, but did not neglect other aspects, and under his leadership a sub-department of Italian was formed in 1957. Bleddyn Roberts, something of an elder stateman on the Arts side, had been Professor of Hebrew and Biblical Studies since 1953 but had been associated with the College since the 1920s. A man with an 'infectious laugh and puckish sense of humour',[15] he had gained recognition for his published work on the Old Testament and the Dead Sea Scrolls. He also ensured that Biblical Studies developed as a thoroughly bilingual department. M. L. Clarke, a much-respected Latinist who published several books on the history of classical studies, served as Vice-Principal in the 1960s. He was also renowned in Bangor for having taken one of the most remarkable catches in the history of the staff cricket team.[16] The College continued, too, to have eminent visiting lecturers. The novelist Irish Murdoch delivered lectures in Bangor in

1962/3, while the great literary critic F. R. Leavis spent a term in Bangor in 1969/70 as a professorial fellow. Lord Denning, the Master of the Rolls, addressed a conference in Bangor in 1967. In the same year the T. Rowland Hughes Art Lecture was given by Sir Anthony Blunt, director of the Courtauld Institute. Blunt was later unmasked as a double agent who had helped the spies Burgess and Maclean to defect to the Soviet Union, and was completely discredited.

Despite its rapid advance in the 1960s, the University College of North Wales appears to have been able to retain its collegiate ethos. The 'swinging sixties' came to Bangor, but in an endearing, home-spun way – epitomized by Georgie Fame and the mildly subversive Johnny Kidd and the Pirates performing in Prichard-Jones Hall just weeks before examinations were sat there. 'Hops' continued to be held (about four each year), the presence of students from the all-female St Mary's College adding spice to dark winter evenings. One student from south Wales, unused to the hilliness of the area, was intrigued to see the lights of St Mary's looking down on Bangor. 'To discover that this College which shone amongst the stars contained only women was an exciting prospect,' he recalled.[17] Soccer matches against the Coleg Normal boys still contained bite in the 1960s, while female students' netball trips to Dublin and Aberystwyth seemed memorable adventures.[18] Controversy erupted with the decision to introduce a bar for students. In April 1963, by a vote of 18 to 11, the College Council agreed in principle to provide a bar in the new refectory, at the request of the Student Representative Council.[19] Non-conformists, already seeing their influence being eroded following the 1960 Licensing Act, were deeply offended by the decision and the College was upbraided by various individuals and groups for many months, including the Gwynedd Temperance Union.[20] Kate Winifred Roberts, a leading figure in Welsh public life and a member of the Council, was an eloquent opponent of the proposal. The majority, however, sided with the students.

For all the academic development and growth, and improvement in the student experience, the challenges of expansion were also making their presence felt. As the growth in student numbers continued at a brisk rate, the Welsh character of the University College appeared to be in retreat. The process had begun in the 1950s. In 1957/8, the year before Charles Evans became Principal, 52 per cent of students were from Wales; at the beginning of the 1950s, the proportion had been 70 per cent. By 1966/7, however, only 24 per cent of Bangor's students came from Wales. This prompted consternation, which coincided with mounting concern in Wales generally over the future of the Welsh language. As early as November 1962, just months after the powerful rallying cry by Saunders Lewis in his radio broadcast, *Tynged yr Iaith* ('The Fate of the Language'), the Cymric Society in the College submitted a petition requesting more extensive use of Welsh in the College. They wanted greater bilingualism in official documents, on signs, notices and circulars. A bilingual covering memorandum argued – with some justification – that 'there is nothing revolutionary in the aims of this petition . . . We are not accusing the College of deliberate disregard or neglect.'[21] Nonetheless, it drew a curt response in English from Principal Evans: he would inform the Senate of the petition, but 'there are normal channels for making the views of students and staff known to the College Authorities'.[22]

Although it conceded relatively minor points, the Senate in 1962/3 was not persuaded that detailed policies or regulations regarding the use of Welsh were either necessary or desirable.[23] In June 1963, the Cymric Society submitted a second memorandum and petition to the Council, calling for more 'Welshness in the life of the College'. To the students, the choice was straightforward: 'either honour the Welsh language or hold it in contempt.'[24] Nor was this solely a student campaign. In the same month, 21 members of the academic staff signed a letter to the Council calling for it to 'give the Welsh language the dignity it deserves'.[25]

In response, the Council appointed a twelve-strong sub-committee – steered by former Principal Sir Emrys Evans – to consider the petition and other submissions. In February 1964, the sub-committee presented its report to the Council. In general, it accepted 'the propriety of the plea advanced that . . . the Welsh language shall receive due recognition in the life and administration of the College'.[26] A more bilingual approach, for example with regard to titles of official publications, College buildings, registration and examination forms, was approved. It was scarcely sufficient, however, for those campaigning for more extensive reform.

These debates were taking place as a fierce storm broke over the future of the University of Wales. Not surprisingly, expansion had fired ambitions for independence amongst some in the University Colleges in Wales. In 1960, the University of Wales Court set up a commission to review the structure and status of the federal University. Divisions quickly emerged on the commission, with a number of Principals – including Charles Evans – favouring the creation of four independent universities in Wales. The 'defederation' issue, as it became known, led to bitter arguments over a lengthy period. In the end, three reports appeared: one, signed by 14 members of the commission, recommended independence for the University Colleges; a second, above the names of 12 commission members, supported the continuation of the federal university. The third, by Principal Thomas Parry of Aberystwyth, advanced the technical argument that the commission should not have made any recommendations.

The controversy raged on campuses and in the columns of newspapers and periodicals such as *Barn*. It was settled only when the University of Wales Court in 1964 accepted the second report and saved the federation. The tensions did not immediately ease, however, for defederation had been widely supported in College Senates. In Bangor, the Senate declared that it 'deplores the action of the University Court in accepting the Second Report', and it called for a Royal Commission to inquire into the matter.[27] The Council was rather more restrained, and after deferring consideration for two meetings, it eventually commented on a limited number of specific points. The affair seemed only to add to growing disharmony in Bangor, for the most forceful supporters of the University of Wales tended to be Welsh staff and Welsh lay Council members. In the end, Charles Evans felt that while it had all revealed major differences, there had been 'no bad blood'.[28]

Moves were also afoot at federal level at this time to foster further teaching through the medium of Welsh. A University of Wales committee recommended the development of Welsh-medium provision, and – interestingly – thought that it should be concentrated in one institution. In a paper to the Bangor Senate in 1966, J. Gwynn Williams and Melville Richards argued that Bangor should be that institution. Both were concerned over the drop in the proportion of

Welsh students in Bangor – 'we are the least "Welsh" of all the Welsh colleges and the most cosmopolitan,' they wrote[29] – and felt that a Welsh-medium programme might help to redress the balance. In fact, the single Welsh-medium college notion was not embraced, and by 1968 appointments were made in both Aberystwyth and Bangor to teach specifically through the medium of Welsh.

The attitude of the University College authorities to the Welsh language was, at best, ambivalent. Charles Evans had used Welsh very little since his childhood, and his confidence in his ability to speak Welsh publicly – possibly lowered by early experiences at Bangor – seemed limited.[30] At any rate, he declined to speak Welsh in public, and spoke only a little in private. Nor was he perceived as showing interest in Welsh culture or in enhancing his own Welsh-language skills. Neither the President, Lord Kenyon, nor the Registrar, Kenneth Lawrence – who appeared to accept greater responsibility as the Principal's health deteriorated – spoke Welsh, and all in all a sympathetic approach to the Welsh language was not very evident.

Skirmishes over the use of Welsh aside, there do not appear to have been in the 1960s the sharp clashes in Bangor which characterized university–student relations elsewhere. Students occasionally flexed their muscles. In 1968/9, a year after moving into the new Union building, students campaigned strongly for greater 'student participation' in College affairs, and eventually gained places on the Council and Senate. In 1970, every student boycotted the refectory for a term, precipitating a radical reorganization of catering. A little later, departmental staff–student committees were also to be formed. Some of the more established academics found it all disconcerting. Commenting on his first experience of a staff–student committee, Clement Mundle, Professor of Philosphy, recounted drily: 'we got a determined young lady who deemed it her duty to reorganize us from scratch'.[31]

Growth and development remained the watchwords as the College entered the 1970s. In 1970, student numbers stood at 2,514, almost double those of 1960. The student population had continued to grow, though at a slower rate than the late 1950s and early 1960s. Indeed, in some subjects, the recruitment of students was becoming a tough assignment, and this led to some structural experiments. Chemistry and Physics graduated 12 and 17 students respectively in 1970/1 (compared with 57 in Electronic Engineering). In that year, it was agreed that they should join forces in a School of Physical and Molecular Sciences spearheaded by two leading scientists, the chemist Charles Stirling and physicist Leslie Wilcock. Mathematics had 12 graduates in 1971, and only three single honours graduates in 1974. In 1973, a School of Mathematics, combining pure and applied aspects of the subject and led by highly regarded mathematicians T. J. M. Boyd and Ronnie Brown, was formed. Greek and Latin fared even worse, with just one graduate between them in 1971. Since the University College's earliest days, each subject had had its own Chair. From 1974, however, when R. E. Wycherley and M. L. Clarke both retired, the two departments were amalgamated under a Professor of Classics, Brian Reardon.

Significant academic reputations continued to be carved out in other departments. Keith Robbins, who was just 31 years old when he was appointed Professor of History in 1971, demonstrated immense promise which he later amply fulfilled, eventually becoming Vice-Chancellor at Lampeter. In Education, J. R. Webster, an Anglesey man who became Professor of Education in 1966 was a stimulating teacher, while Aled Eames, another contender for the Education Chair, devoted his attention to the maritime history of north Wales, at which he excelled. Jimmy Dodd, a zoologist whose interests were predominantly marine, and Tony Fogg, a botanist with a passionate interest in Antarctica who came to strengthen the plant side of Marine Biology, made hugely distinguished contributions in their fields. Ian Lucas (Agriculture) and Laurence Roche (Forestry) re-emphasized the international aspects of their subjects through major research projects in Saudi Arabia and Nigeria respectively.

New academic directions continued to be mapped out. A Masters degree in Social Work was a noteworthy addition in 1971/2. Under Jack Revell, Professor of Economics and a convinced Marxist, a Masters degree in Financial Economics – the beginning of a specialism in banking and finance – was introduced in 1970, while a new degree in Accounting commenced in 1974. Tim Miles, in the Psychology Department, pioneered research into dyslexia, and a Dyslexia Unit was formally recognized in 1976/7. Drama grew stronger, and a separate department and Chair in the subject were established in 1976. The College infrastructure continued to develop, though in a somewhat piecemeal fashion. The Brambell laboratories were opened in 1971 by Lord Zuckerman – the external appearance of the building arousing, as the new Zoology Professor Jimmy Dodd remarked, 'mixed reactions'.[32] A theatre had been planned for a number of years, and Theatr Gwynedd – built (somewhat over budget) with the backing of local authorities and various trusts as well as the Welsh Arts Council – opened its doors in January 1975. A sports centre on the Ffriddoedd site was completed in 1976/7, while modern residential accommodation (a 'bedsitter block', named Llys Tryfan) also came on stream.

The economic temperature, however, stoked by the oil crisis of 1973 and an alarming inflation rate, was rising. Asked by the UGC in 1973 for a ten-year development plan, Charles Evans postulated growth to 4,500 students by 1981/2, though only if there were adequate funding for buildings and equipment.[33] Between 1974 and 1976 the financial situation was discouraging. The UGC visited the College in 1975/6 and provided 'encouragement and helpful advice, but little comfort'.[34] Moreover, students generally were becoming more vociferous. At various points in the early 1970s they railed against the funding of the Students' Union, hall fees and cutbacks. The Principal had little sympathy with the political activities of students, commenting acidly, when they protested about student grants in 1973/4, on their 'irresponsible interference in the College's normal working'.[35]

Resentment over the enlargement of the College still simmered. In 1971, 25 Welsh members of staff (including a number of future Professors) had submitted a memorandum to the College Court objecting to the continued growth.[36] It was a well-argued document, but it was not taken up by the Court, and some academics on the Senate profoundly disagreed with their colleagues' analysis. Student numbers continued to climb, and stood at 2,814 in 1975, but the proportion of Welsh students remained stubbornly at 25 per cent. One notable step was the creation of a Welsh hall of residence. After extensive discussion in a Council sub-committee, and a survey of the demand for such accommodation, in May 1973 the Council decided that 'University Hall' should be transformed into a mixed hall for Welsh-speaking students. In October 1974 the Welsh hall opened with 153 students and was named, appropriately, 'Neuadd John Morris-Jones'.

Feelings persisted in some sections of the University College that Welsh candidates for senior academic positions were being overlooked. Particular disquiet emerged in 1973 with the appointment of a non Welsh-speaker – Max Wilcox, an Australian academic who joined Bangor from the University of Newcastle – to the Chair of Biblical Studies in succession to Bleddyn Jones Roberts. Both students and organizations such as the Union of Welsh Independents expressed dismay, but the Council seemed unmoved by such views.[37]

Sir Charles Evans was aware of the rumblings of discontent, but he remained firmly wedded to a policy of expansion. Writing in the student newspaper *Forecast* in early 1974, he was unequivocal: 'a refusal to grow at a time when funds and suitably qualified applicants for entry were forthcoming' would damage the College. 'I believe that the Universities have a duty to try to find places for all those who wish to enter and who are likely to profit by the university experience,' he continued. The Principal did not beat his breast too strongly over the critics of expansion, noting that students had demonstrated 'not very whole-heartedly, I think, against it'.[38]

Later that year, a sudden squall over a different aspect of expansion seemed to stain further the University College's reputation. The back-drop was a government White Paper on the integration of Colleges of Education which trained teachers within universities. It seemed particularly pertinent to the small city of Bangor where two such colleges – Coleg Normal and St Mary's College – existed cheek by jowl with the University College. In June 1974, Sir Charles Evans introduced a discussion paper at the College Council on the possible amalgamation of both St Mary's and Coleg Normal within the University College of North Wales. The Council – on which the Principal of Coleg Normal, J. A. Davies, sat – officially welcomed the document. Discussions between the parties were suggested, and the Council set up a committee of negotiators after the UGC had signalled support for such a move. The initial signs were mixed: the governors of St Mary's College were content to proceed with integration; it made a good deal of sense to this small college linked to the Church in Wales. But the local education authorities in north Wales were unambiguously opposed to any integration involving Coleg Normal, although academic staff of the Normal at one point stated their support for the establishment in Bangor of an 'integrated bilingual School of Education'.[39]

In truth, many inside and outside Coleg Normal viewed the whole affair with suspicion. The apparently towering growth that had already taken place in the University College generated a certain vulnerability on the part of partner organizations. Moreover, although modest advances in Welsh-medium provision in the University College had taken place – by 1974/5 there were thirteen staff appointed specifically to teach through the medium of Welsh – the leaders of the two institutions were unlikely to share the same vision for Welsh-medium education and the Welsh language.

It was not long before a political salvo was fired. On 11 June 1975, during a debate of the Welsh Grand Committee, more than one member of parliament voiced concern over the amalgamation proposals. The MP for Montgomeryshire, Emlyn Hooson, was reported as referring to 'empire-building' by the University College and its Education Department. Some other attacks on the academic reputation of UCNW were reported, stinging Sir Charles Evans into an indignant reply. 'There is no foundation for such damaging and irresponsible words,' he protested in a letter to all members of the Welsh Grand Committee.[40] The Principal asserted vigorously that the initiative for the integration proposals had stemmed from the government, not from the University College or from any scheme for aggrandizement. At a College Council meeting on 25 June, J. A. Davies, the Principal of Coleg Normal, referred to the embarrassment caused to Coleg Normal by the Welsh Grand Committee debate, and made it clear that 'the statements did not emanate from the Normal College'.[41] Later the governors of Coleg Normal endorsed Principal Davies's comments.

Nonetheless, the amalgamation proposals involving Coleg Normal had effectively been scuppered. The government formally requested that discussions take place, but early in 1976 the Secretary of State for Wales informed the University College that he had decided that Coleg Normal should remain in existence as a 'free-standing teacher training institution'.[42] It was to be another 20 years before integration between Coleg Normal and the University became a reality. Discussions with St Mary's College were relatively unproblematic, and in June 1976 the Council approved the incorporation of St Mary's within the University College from September 1977.

The Coleg Normal episode had been unfortunate. There is no doubt that the impetus for the proposed realignment derived from government policy, and the University College was, on occasion, unfairly maligned. Yet it had not always provided the most congenial public image, and its presentation of its case was perhaps not as subtle as it might have been. There may have been qualms about the University College's commitment to Welsh-medium study. Coming as it did, on top of growing financial concerns and mounting criticism of the College's attitude to expansion and to Welsh-language issues, the affair did little to enhance its prestige. In fact, damaging fault-lines were opening up.

33. A pencil drawing by John Merton of Charles Evans, Principal 1958–1984

34. Lord Hailsham (right) during the opening of the new Physics Building in 1962

35. Bertolt Brecht's *The Tutor* performed by the English Dramatic Society in 1965

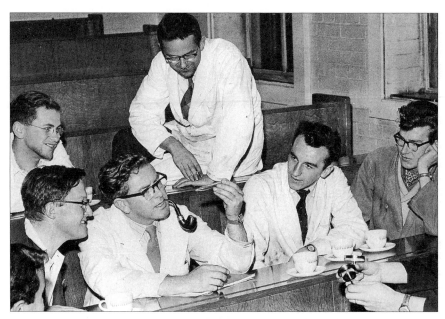

36. W. Charles Evans (with pipe) holds forth to postgraduate students and researchers in Biochemistry – one, Douglas Ribbons (second from right) later occupied the Chair of Biochemistry and Soil Science

37. Students' Union Executive, 1963/4, in the Council Chamber

38. Dennis Crisp, one of the world's most influential
marine scientists, in the 1960s

39. J. Gwynn Williams, Professor of Welsh History,
and Vice-Principal from 1974 until 1979

40. William Mathias (left), Professor of Music, with Gordon Lamb, visiting Head of Department from the University of Texas in 1976

41. Bedwyr Lewis Jones, Professor of Welsh from 1973 until 1992

42. Students of Neuadd John Morris-Jones and Welsh-medium
teaching staff in the early 1980s

43. Principal Sir Charles Evans (left), Lord Kenyon, President (centre), and
Eric Hughes, Registrar, at a meeting of the Court in the late 1970s

44. Student protesters gather, watched by police officers, in
January 1979

45. The College rugby team, 1979/80

6

'We are drifting into very perilous waters' Confrontation and Crisis, 1976–1984

As the squabbles over the integration of the Colleges of Education were dying away, the Council received, in June 1976, a document from the Cymric Society of Welsh students outlining requests for an increase in the use of Welsh in the College. The Council's reaction was to agree that the matter should be debated at its next meeting in October.[1] When the Council meeting took place on 27 October, three representatives of the society were allowed into the Council Chamber to put their case, following a slight disturbance outside the door. Essentially, they wanted a clear language policy. The Council felt it could not accept the Cymric Society's document 'as it stands', but they agreed to set up a sub-committee, chaired by the President, Lord Kenyon, to review the bilingual policy.[2]

Council members may not have realized it, but they were sitting on a powder keg. Their seemingly cautious, procedural approach did not exactly win plaudits amongst the Welsh students. On 11 November 1976, the College's Academic Registry offices were occupied by students and some damage occurred; slogans were painted on walls around the Main Building, and some notices were removed from walls and burned in the main quadrangle. On 15 November, the Finance Office was entered, and boxes and files were scattered over the floor. The Cymric Society accepted responsibility for these demonstrations, and an apology was conveyed to one officer in the Finance Office whom they felt sympathized with their arguments. The 'unconstitutional' methods used by the students appalled Sir Charles Evans and other senior colleagues. On 15 November too, the Senate took decisive action: four student officers of the Cymric Society were suspended for the remainder of the 1976/7 academic year.

Battle lines were now being drawn. On 22 November, some 600–800 students marched through Bangor and were addressed in the main quadrangle by the campaigner and singer, Dafydd Iwan. The next day, Cymric members staged a sit-in in the new Arts section of the Main Building, and blocked the quadrangle car park. The College authorities applied for a High Court order to be served on the students. It was granted on 27 November, and the building was repossessed the following day. Locally, the students attracted much support, and over 150 letters backing their action were received by the College. Some Welsh academics were sympathetic, and certain lay Council members expressed concerns over the College's actions: O. V. Jones, a Welsh-speaking obstetrician and a senior Council member, was 'very unhappy about the harsh penalty given to the four students'.[3] On the other hand, some academics were outraged by the students' conduct. The Bangor branch of the lecturers' union, the AUT, called for 'firm disciplinary action to be taken',[4] while the *Caernarfon and Denbigh Herald* in an editorial declared itself 'glad that the principal of Bangor University College was firm in his handling of some students'.[5]

When the Council met on 8 December 1976, levels of anxiety were rising perceptibly. After a short debate, and on a motion proposed by the Archbishop of Wales, G. O. Williams, and seconded by O. V. Jones, the Council deplored the use of violence, and called on the Cymric Society to refrain from disruptive action. But it also asked the Senate – which was responsible for student discipline – to show clemency. On 15 December, the Senate reconsidered the matter, and 'as a special act of clemency' lifted the suspensions on the four students, on condition that undertakings were given by the students and by Cymric that they would refrain from disruptive actions. The immediate conflict seemed to have passed. Sir Thomas Parry, former Principal of

Aberystwyth and now a resident in Bangor, was 'very glad indeed' about the Senate decision, and hoped that the students would 'suitably reciprocate'.[6] They did so: the required undertakings were forthcoming.

Meanwhile, the Bilingual Policy Review was making modest but undramatic progress. An interim document at the December Council meeting in 1976 reported that information was being gathered, and that the Senate was being asked to consider proposals regarding bilingualism and the College Prospectus. Relations between the College and Welsh students remained somewhat fractious. In April 1977, certain students interrupted a conference of headteachers in the College, prompting exasperation amongst some senior academics. The Senate again prepared to act: one suspension was imposed, followed by a second ten days later. But student opinion was rapidly hardening. 'We have grown extremely tired of receiving a few crumbs from the College from time to time,' wrote three students from Neuadd John Morris-Jones. 'Punishment will not keep us quiet'.[7] In September 1977, the Council approved a report of its Bilingual Policy Review Committee, and decided that a meeting should be arranged with four members of the Cymric Society who had given evidence to the Committee. The University of Wales Court then decided to have its say, expressing regret over the differences which had emerged between the College and the students, and hope that the problems would be overcome 'through a positive approach towards the Welsh language' and the implementation of an 'official College bilingual policy' in each constituent college of the federal University.[8]

If College leaders hoped that the student campaign would fizzle out, they were mistaken. Indeed, dissension increased throughout 1978, with numerous disturbances across the campus: in February, locks on doors in 'professors' corridor' of the Main Building were tampered with; an attempt to jam the College's switchboard was made. The student accommodation office was also entered and some documents removed: on this occasion, the police were called and three students later appeared in court, although the judge directed a verdict of 'not guilty'.

In November 1978, an active 'Dim Ehangu' ('No Expansion') poster campaign was set in motion by students. A blockade of the Main

Quadrangle car park took place and smoke bombs were released near the Main Building. A demonstration took place in the Library on 16 November. The College authorities reacted as they had on previous similar occasions. Four Welsh students were brought before a Board of Discipline, and charges of misconduct against three of them were substantiated. This provoked the most serious clash ever witnessed in the University College. On 11 December 1978, a student occupation of the Academic Registry and parts of the new Arts section of the Main Building was initiated. Lectures could not take place, and numerous administrative members of staff had to be temporarily re-located. There was considerable turmoil, and many staff held their breath. The University College immediately sought a court order to regain possession of the building. When, after several days, students were forced to vacate the building, several thousand personal student files were found to have been removed from the Academic Registry, together with some UCCA application forms and other documents. The police were informed; some students involved were identified by various means, and disciplinary charges were brought against ten students. When the disciplinary hearings took place, a number of students effectively had 20-month suspensions imposed: they could not return to the College until October 1980. Appeals were lodged, and campaigns in support of the suspended students – including a march into a meeting of the College Court – were waged. The Senate's Appeal Board – which met on several occasions early in 1979 – was, on the whole, unmoved.

Feelings were now running high on all sides. Undoubtedly a serious breach of regulations had occurred, and University College leaders were genuinely alarmed at this turn of events and at the scale and force of the action taken by students. Some senior academics on the Senate were incensed at the student activities. In January 1979, the Principal wrote to all members of staff explaining the situation and urging them not to retaliate with physical action.[9] Non-professorial staff, too, expressed their concern over the 'use of disruptive tactics'.[10] But cross-currents were also appearing. A number of academic and support staff sympathized with the student cause if not, perhaps, with all the methods used. Staff in the Cylch y Darlithwyr Cymraeg (Circle of Welsh Lecturers) wanted channels of communication opened up with the Welsh students, who had formed Undeb Myfyr-wyr Colegau Bangor (UMCB) (Union of Students of Bangor Colleges). Indeed, longstanding friendships between senior academics, who found themselves holding differing views in this dispute, came under great strain during this period. Certain members of the College Court also spoke up in favour of the cause which the protesters es-poused: in December 1978, the Court officially expressed concern over the policy of expansion.[11]

Bedwyr Lewis Jones, Professor of Welsh and Head of the Depart-ment in which a number of the student protestors studied, endeav-oured to ease the tension. In a private letter to Sir Charles Evans, he attempted to persuade the Principal to adopt a less confrontational stance, and to try to understand the student viewpoint. He was bluntly critical of the leadership of the College: at Court meetings, he told Sir Charles, 'there is a lack of rapport between the platform and the floor. Too many matters become confrontations.'[12] He did not condone the use of force, but he did press for UMCB to be recognized as a student organization and for greater communication between the College and students. The Professor of Welsh received scant reward for his efforts. He endured some virulent attacks from certain students whom he had tried to help – a situation which hurt him deeply – and the Principal did not modify his stance. Fissures appeared, too, in the student community. The Students' Union, the officially recognized student organization, condemned the disruptive activities that had taken place.[13] Even amongst Welsh-speaking students, there were some who felt that some protestors had gone too far. The President of Plaid Cymru, Gwynfor Evans, grew concerned over the situation in Bangor and the attitude of some Bangor students, and he wrote to one of the campaigners.[14]

The official line taken by the University College was not altogether a surprise. The student protesters were 'fanatical militants', in the Principal's view,[15] and should be brought to justice. The College leadership had actually changed little since the initial petitions from the Cymric Society in the early and mid-1960s. The President, Lord Kenyon, and the Principal, Sir Charles Evans, remained in place, although Eric Hughes had replaced Kenneth Lawrence as Registrar in 1974. The Vice-Principal since 1974 had been J. Gwynn Williams,

Professor of Welsh History and a strong advocate of bilingual policies and of Welsh-medium study. As the confrontation between the students and the College authorities intensified, Gwynn Williams found himself in the acutely difficult position of being the University's disciplinary officer. He carried out his duty of presenting the cases against the students charged, and he clearly believed that, as regulations had been breached, students found guilty of a breach should be punished. But he was disquieted by the severity of the penalties imposed by the Board of Discipline. He wrote privately to Sir Charles Evans to say that he was 'greatly dismayed' by the decisions of the Appeal Board in February 1979. 'The Appeal Board was immovable,' he protested, 'and this only two days after the College had been charged with the task of healing and settling.' The sentences, he argued, 'cannot command the assent of moderate opinion'.[16] Gwynn Williams, however, found himself the target of criticism from some members of staff.

Prior to this, Bedwyr Lewis Jones had tried to moderate the attitude of the Appeal Board. In February, he wrote to the Board – which included many of his academic colleagues on the Senate – making a plea that the suspended students be allowed to return in October 1979 rather than October 1980. Some of the penalties he thought 'extremely harsh'.[17] After the appeals had been rejected, the arguments continued to excite indignation. During the night of 3–4 March 1979, serious damage was done to the Library catalogue and records. In April, Bedwyr Lewis Jones again wrote to the Principal in support of the original suspended students, and enclosing the signatures of students and staff in his department who took a similar view. Sir Charles Evans, although he reported the existence of the letter to the Council and the Senate, was not going to waver: 'I am sorry that your Department takes this attitude,' was his only response.[18]

In fact, by this time, the most discordant – and the most fateful – note in this whole affair had been struck. The Vice-Principal, Gwynn Williams, had become increasingly concerned about key aspects of the dispute: the fortuitous nature of detection in the few cases brought before the Board of Discipline; the severity of the punishment meted out; and the apparent unwillingness of the Appeal Board to consider pleas in mitigation. In March, J. Gwynn Williams asked to be relieved of those duties of the Vice-Principal which related to student discipline. He was content to continue with other duties as a Vice-Principal, and was of course aware there was a second Vice-Principal, Ian Stephenson, a Professor in Electronic Engineering, who might have been willing to take on the disciplinary role. These suggestions seemed not to sway the Principal. About three weeks later, in a terse conversation in Sir Charles Evans's car in the car park, the Principal indicated that if Gwynn Williams could not discharge his disciplinary duties, he could no longer continue as Vice-Principal.[19] J. Gwynn Williams therefore resigned as Vice-Principal, and explained his position in a letter to the Council on 18 April 1979. He ended it by expressing the hope that those who held moderate views would 'find it easier than I have done to build bridges in this College'.[20] The Council received his resignation 'with regret' and expressed 'complete confidence' in the way that he had discharged his duties.[21] (He was to return to the Council in later years and become Vice-President.)

This was high drama indeed. At the height of the conflict with a section of the student community, a leading member of the University, the Vice-Principal, had resigned, essentially over the treatment of the students. J. Gwynn Williams, a meticulous scholar who thought deeply about the College's place in history, was neither incautious nor given to extravagant gestures. He had never previously resigned from any body. 'I do so now only because I must,' he wrote privately to a colleague.[22] By this time, the unrest in the University College was front-page news almost daily – in UK as well as Welsh newspapers – and frequently featured on radio and television news bulletins. Local councillors and Westminster politicians publicly voiced alarm. In late 1979, an attempt to raise the stakes was made by Lady Eirene White, a former member of parliament and daughter of Thomas Jones (Lloyd George's confidant). She and Wallis Evans proposed a motion at the Court, asking the Pro-Chancellor of the federal University, Lord Edmund-Davies, to intervene in the College and discuss measures 'to abate the present discontent'.[23] J. Gwynn Williams understood their concern, but recognized that this would not be a constitutionally appropriate step.[24] In fact, Lord Edmund-Davies quite properly declined to act. In the meantime, something approaching pitched battles between the College authorities and the students continued, and disruption (marches, slogans painted on buildings, blocked car parks) seemed a routine part of campus life.

Despite many months of turbulence, it must be said that much of the ordinary work of the College continued. Student numbers remained high, at over 3,000 in total between 1976 and 1979 (though they were to dip in 1979/80). Academic departments endeavoured to focus on their discipline and the needs of students, and some important initiatives were taken. In 1978/9 the Chair in Drama was occupied by Michael Anderson. In Electronic Engineering, a pioneering M.Eng. programme was introduced after the University College had been selected by GEC-Marconi Electronics and Ferranti Ltd as the institution in Wales at which they wished to support such a development. Other new professorial appointments – such as Iolo Wyn Williams (Education), Roy King (Social Theory and Institutions), Geoffrey Hunter (Philosophy) and Martin Smith (Classics) – were made, while Alwyn Roberts, previously of the Social Theory and Institutions Department, became Director of Extra-Mural Studies in succession to Alun Llywelyn-Williams. In 1979, the University College of North Wales was able to boast of the presence of five Fellows of the Royal Society amongst the 16 science Professors – an astonishingly high proportion: John Harper, Jimmy Dodd, Dennis Crisp, Tony Fogg and W. Charles Evans. In 1980/1, William Mathias, Professor of Music, gained considerable international prestige when he was invited to compose music for the wedding of the Prince and Princess of Wales.

Nonetheless, problems were mounting on all fronts. The financial position of the University College, in particular, had been weakening markedly. In 1979, Sir Charles Evans admitted that 'we are struggling to maintain our standards of work in the face of grave financial shortage'.[25] Financial deficits had been recorded in each of the three years from 1977/8. The Conservative Government of the day appeared in a mood to rein in universities. Gloom was settling on the higher education sector, and early retirement schemes began to be formulated. In June 1981, Sir Edward Parkes, chair of the UGC, visited Bangor and warned that the institution would not 'escape the forthcoming financial cuts'.[26] The following month, the UGC delivered a crippling blow. An average cut of 18 per cent in university budgets across the UK was announced. For Bangor, with its other political and managerial problems, the news was dispiriting in the extreme. The College's grant for the next three years suggested a deficit of nearly £2million (in a total expenditure of around £13 million) if no corrective action were taken. Sir Charles Evans hoped that voluntary retirements could be secured, but he declared that redundancies may be unavoidable. 'The prospect is dark,' he wrote, 'but it is not hopeless provided we steel ourselves to accept hardships.'[27]

Even before UGC's momentous July 1981 letter, the political situation in the College had reached boiling point. On 13 April 1981, 14 senior academics (12 professors and two other department heads) signed a letter to the President, Lord Kenyon, asserting that the Principal could no longer 'carry the burden' of leadership. 'There is a widespread feeling at the moment,' they reported, 'that we are drifting into very perilous waters without any clear sense of purpose and direction.'[28] Non-professorial staff also put in writing their concern 'over the present leadership'.[29]

Sir Charles Evans had long been confined to a wheelchair. His ability to travel was limited (which prompted comment over his attendance at meetings away from Bangor), and he was seen less frequently in the College than in earlier years. His illness meant inevitably declining physical powers, and there is little doubt that by the end of the 1970s he felt intensely the daily weight and pressure of his position. In the midst of the student problems, in January 1979, he declined an invitation from his old friend Anne McCandless to a party, confiding privately that 'anything like that now takes me an awful lot of time and arrangement'. 'If I look at an old diary,' he continued, 'I am shaken by how much I could once do in a day compared with even ten years ago – and I certainly haven't speeded up in the last ten years.'[30] He increasingly endured attacks from several quarters, though he rarely responded forcefully and rarely modified his position. He held firm to his view that what the College had experienced was 'wanton efforts at disruption by small groups of misguided people'.[31] To many, however, his earlier virtues – determination, bravery – were increasingly coming to be seen as rigidity and stubbornness.

Lord Kenyon was clearly concerned over the developing situation, and he consulted his Vice-Presidents, O. V. Jones and Sir Elwyn Jones. The President's own position was not unquestioned. In February

1981, an attempt was made at the Council to elect him Chair of Council for one meeting only; in the event, he was elected for the year, but Kenyon made it clear that he would give way if the Council wished to replace him.[32] His reaction to the letter from 14 academics was to invite J. Gwynn Williams, the former Vice-Principal and one of the signatories, to broker a confidential meeting between the President, the Vice-Presidents and the senior staff who had written to him. When the meeting took place in June 1981, the academics pulled no punches: they wanted 'a leader of vision, energy and enthusiasm to pilot the College through this crucial transitional period'.[33] Lord Kenyon decided to see the Principal at once, and conveyed to him the views which had been expressed. He reported within days that 'it is not Sir Charles's intention to make any statement of his future at this moment in time.'[34]

After the meeting with the President, the 14 senior staff members stepped up their campaign. On 9 June, they sent a candid letter to all Senate members explaining the action they had taken. They believed that the Principal 'ought now to be persuaded to retire',[35] pointing out that he was now out of day-to-day working contact with academic departments and staff. The strength of feeling on this matter could not be disguised, and it was paraded dramatically at a momentous Council meeting later that month. On 24 June 1981, two motions were placed before the Council: one, above the signatures of some lay Council members, and framed in a general context, asked the Principal 'to contemplate his personal position' in the light of the virulence of the crisis facing higher education; a second, from some of the professors, but also signed by some non-professorial staff members, asserted pointedly that Sir Charles Evans 'is not able to perform his functions adequately'.[36] Following a tense debate, the motion from lay members was passed by 25 votes to 18, and the Council formally asked the Principal to consider his position. The second motion was then not put to the Council.

It was a grave step, and the University College had truly reached a point of crisis. Sir Charles Evans was indignant at this turn of events. He bitterly resented the fact that senior colleagues had held discussions behind closed doors and that leaks to the press had occurred. Nor was he in a totally solitary position. In July, the Vice-Principals, Ian Stephenson and Jack Revell (together with the Vice-Principal-elect,

Geoff Sagar) wrote to academic colleagues urging them to support the Principal. In August 1981, another group of senior members of staff (including 14 other professors, a Dean and two Heads of Department) wrote to Lord Kenyon in support of Sir Charles Evans. 'We believe that it is in the best interests of the College for the Principal to remain at our head, and for the College to be united behind him'.[37]

Sir Charles Evans now faced an unprecedented level of criticism and difficulty. But he had faced difficulty for many years, and even at the age of 63, he was not a man to give in easily. In October 1981, he gave the Council his response: he would neither resign nor retire. He deplored the 'underhand nature' of the campaign mounted against him and the situation in which the University College found itself – 'a state of affairs which would be made worse by me giving in'. 'I can assure the Council,' he concluded, 'that I shall retire when the time is right.'[38] In a thunderously defiant message, he quoted Milton's *Samson Agonistes*: 'My heels are fetterd, but my fist is free.'[39] The statement was 'received' by the Council.[40]

For a short period, attention was being diverted to the desperate financial position, and to the early retirement scheme. The UGC had ordered a significant decrease in Bangor's student numbers, and recommended discussions about subject rationalization in Wales. In a decidedly interventionist approach, the UGC advocated transferring Statistics and Computing Science to Aberystwyth, with Applied Mathematics courses coming in the opposite direction. Sir Charles Evans felt Bangor had been harshly treated, and protested about the decrease in student numbers. 'I do feel that Bangor has been relatively hard hit', he told the UGC Chair.[41] In May 1982, the UGC lessened the blow slightly by agreeing to increase numbers in science by 60, but this did little to ease the seriousness of the College's position.

By the autumn of 1981, plans to shed staff were well advanced. In a rather indiscriminate approach, aided by generous compensation supported by the UGC, virtually any member of staff who wished to retire was allowed to do so. By September 1982, around 70 members of staff had agreed to depart, many of them experienced and influential academics and officers. They included six professors, the Librarian Glyn Heywood, the Accountant Joe Cherry and the Buildings Officer Howard Slade. The following year, a further seven professors retired. By 1984, 128 staff in all had left. It was a sweeping set of departures of senior personnel, but it helped to stave off a financial catastrophe.

Eight months after his statement to the Council, in June 1982, Sir Charles Evans announced his intention to retire in September 1984.[42] In fact, this meant that he would remain in office until nearly one year after his 65th birthday – the point when he would be required to retire. In October 1982, Lord Kenyon was effectively forced out. He was nominated for re-election as President by Sir Charles Evans and four colleagues; however, an alternative nominee – Sir William Mars-Jones – was put forward. In the resulting ballot, Sir William received the most votes. Two months later, therefore, Lord Kenyon relinquished the Presidency after 35 years, having shown, in the Principal's view – and that of others – 'the finest qualities expected of that office'.[43] In 1983, Eric Hughes, a loyal and respected Registrar who disliked the acrimonious atmosphere that had developed in the College, retired. Slowly but surely, the senior officers of the University College were leaving the stage.

Controversy over the management of the University College was not yet over, for another furious quarrel blew up when the Council refused to endorse the appointment of a non Welsh-speaking Registrar. Eight candidates were originally interviewed in May 1982 for the post, but the selection committee felt unable to recommend a candidate for appointment. In January 1983 the post was readvertised and the selection committee, led by the new Chair of Council, O. V. Jones, interviewed 13 applicants (including six who were Welsh speaking). In March 1983, the committee recommended the appointment of Frederick Smyth, then Registrar and Deputy Secretary at Stirling and a non Welsh-speaker. Thirteen Council members forced an extraordinary meeting to debate the recommendation, and by 29 votes to 12, the Council decided not to proceed with the appointment, agreeing that it would be more appropriate to wait until a new Principal had been appointed.[44]

The Council had appointed an Acting Registrar, Gwyn R. Thomas, in December 1982, and ultimately he was confirmed in post. There was force in the argument that an appointment should first be made to the Principalship, but the Council's rejection of the selection committee's recommendation enraged some senior figures and placed the Principal and the Chair of Council in a highly embarrassing situation. The Chair, O. V. Jones, announced that he would have to review his personal position, though he was later dissuaded from resignation. But it was yet another clash, at the heart of which was the University College's attitude to the Welsh language.

These were dark and divisive days, the darkest in the University's history. There were many during the late 1970s and early 1980s who seriously doubted whether the University College of North Wales would survive. Even a quarter of a century later, recollections of the events of 1978–84 are capable of generating heat and acrimony. A coolly objective assessment is neither simple nor uncontentious. In all probability, the expansion of the University College, given the tenor of UK public policy on universities and higher education, was inevitable. What might have been played differently in Bangor was the attitude to the Welsh identity, language and culture. By the mid-1970s, however, the time for understanding and consensus on this matter had passed. A more flexible approach at an earlier stage – at the beginning of the 1960s – might have averted the worst of the arguments. What seems certain is that the reputation of the University College was seriously impaired; and that the subsequent development of more comprehensive bilingual policies from the mid-1980s would not have taken place if the battles over the language had not occurred.

So, after more than a quarter of a century, Sir Charles Evans's principalship came to a bitter and querulous end. There were colleagues who steadfastly supported him to the end: the University College had grown markedly and had initiated many new developments during his years in office; pure academic successes were not inconsiderable. To others, he had shown a cold indifference to the Welsh language and culture, and was unsuited to the modern requirements of university management. In private he could display great courtesy and humanity to those in a difficult situation – for example, to unsuccessful candidates for posts. Yet he could also appear sharply insensitive to the feelings of others. He was self-effacing, rejecting approaches from authors who wished to write his biography: 'although I've had an enjoyable life, I hardly think it would serve as an inspiration to anyone,' he wrote in 1975.[45] But he could also be autocratic and unbending.

He had little liking for the social side of campus life, and seemed uncomfortable having to forge the political and personal relationships increasingly necessary to support institutional advance.

Sir Charles was granted two months' leave of absence and effectively retired in July 1984. He met his successor, but made no attempt to brief or influence him in a particular direction. At his last Council meeting in June 1984, the Council recorded, in a perfunctory way, 'its thanks to Sir Charles Evans for his long service as Principal'.[46] (In October, after he had departed, the Council minuted a slightly more detailed tribute.) He spent his last day in office at the Principal's residence at Bryn Haul. One or two of the College's senior administrative officers and close colleagues called to pay their respects. Just weeks before the University College of North Wales was due to celebrate its centenary, Sir Charles Evans left office and never again had any contact with the University College of which he had been head for 26 years.

'I am sure that a radical approach is right'
Responding to Change, 1984–2009

The year 1984 was, on more than one count, a critical juncture in the history of the University College of North Wales. It marked, first and foremost, the centenary of the institution, which helpfully provided a break in the clouds, an opportunity to breathe again. There were formal celebrations in October 1984 – including a procession to the remains of the Penrhyn Arms, and the presentation to the University College of an impressive mace by the Old Students' Association – and the launch of a new appeal, facilitated by the foundation of a Development Trust. There were social occasions too, including a staff tea, which helped wounds to be healed and divides to be bridged. In many respects, the centenary events enabled a line to be drawn in the sand.

Most decisive of all, of course, was the change in the leadership of the University College. The new Principal, Eric Sunderland, who had been Professor of Anthropology at Durham for thirteen years and a Pro Vice-Chancellor for five, had initially been ambivalent about the post when it was advertised. His family was settled in Durham – although he had been approached about various positions in Oxford – and he had little direct knowledge of Bangor or its recent turbulent events. He was, however, a Welshman: he hailed from Ammanford, and both he and his wife had close relatives in south Wales.[1] After what seemed like a curious appointment process, he accepted the challenge and took office just weeks before the official centenary celebrations.

The University College had made an astute choice. Eric Sunderland appeared to be the very antithesis of Sir Charles Evans. He had extensive academic and administrative experience, having worked at Durham continuously since 1958, had been a Head of Department and had risen to the position of Pro Vice-Chancellor; he was a fluent Welsh speaker, who made a point early in his Principalship of meeting and speaking to students in Neuadd John Morris-Jones; moreover, he was notably at ease in social gatherings and set considerable store by the public and ambassadorial aspects of the Principal's role. He was fortunate in being able to identify a small team of senior colleagues who were to provide staunch support and complementary experience. These included Geoff Sagar, Professor of Agricultural Botany and an experienced navigator of committees, who had been Vice-Principal since 1981; and Alwyn Roberts, the Director of Extra-Mural Studies, who had wide public experience, having served as Principal of Pachhunga Government College in India, as a member of Gwynedd County Council and as a governor of the BBC as well as a senior lecturer in Social Theory and Institutions.

The Presidency had already been settled in October 1982, when Sir William Mars-Jones, a High Court judge, had succeeded Lord Kenyon. Sir William, who had grown up in Llansannan in Denbighshire, was the first Welsh-speaking President in the University College's history – although his appointment was opposed by the Welsh students of UMCB. The Vice-Presidents in 1984 were Emyr Wyn Jones and Edward Rees and, in 1985, John Howard Davies, a former Director of Education who was to become Chair of S4C the following year, became Chair of the College Council. All in all, the tone and the personnel in the higher echelons of the University College had dramatically changed.

Certainly a climate was being created in which a more positive approach to the Welsh language could evolve. The Council was proactive in ensuring that a more extensive bilingual policy developed, setting up its own standing bilingual policy committee. In 1986, too, a School of Welsh-Medium Studies, which drew together staff who

taught or had interests in Welsh-medium courses, was formally insti-
tuted. Its first Director was Gwyn Thomas, a Professor in the Welsh
Department and a poet of considerable distinction whose accessible
poetry depicting modern situations was a major influence on a new
generation of poets. In other respects, too, the University College
seemed slowly to be recovering its self-confidence. In June 1984,
following a UGC review, Bangor was selected as one of two university
centres in the UK for the study of Oceanography (the other centre
was Southampton); resources were to be directed accordingly.[2] The
centenary appeal, too, was able to declare after one year that its target
of raising £1 million had been reached: a particularly noteworthy
contribution was a major donation from Sheikh Yamani, the Saudi
Arabian Oil Minister, to promote research in the newly formed
Centre for Arid Zone Studies.[3] The Economics Department secured
sponsorship for both staff and students from the National Westminster Bank, the first step in the development of a fruitful relationship with major banking organizations.

For all these heartening indicators, there were also worrying signs.
The UGC in 1985 was intently preparing the university sector for
deeper cutbacks in funding. Universities were told to expect an average reduction in funding of 2 per cent per annum until the end of
the decade. Plans for dealing with this situation were called for from
all universities by November 1985. The College Court thought that
this would do 'irreparable harm',[4] while Eric Sunderland stated
clearly that 'economies must immediately be effected'.[5] A small planning committee was formed, and some tough choices were made:
the teaching of Classics and of Italian was to cease; a School of Ocean
Sciences, merging Marine Biology and Oceanography, would be
formed to build on acknowledged strengths; and extensive physical restructuring would take place to reduce costs. There was a grim realism
about the University College's reaction, but few suspected just how
rough a ride the College would receive.

The University College's plan, when it was submitted in November
1985, seemed to cut little ice with the UGC. When funding for 1986/7
was announced in the spring of 1986, Bangor was handed an actual
reduction of 0.5 per cent in its grant, which in real terms amounted
to a 5 per cent cut. It was an 'extremely serious' situation, as the

Principal reported to the Council,[6] and a substantial deficit was projected. A meeting to discuss matters between officers of the University College and the UGC was set for 7 July 1986. When it occurred, the College officers were told bluntly that their 1985 plan, despite its unpalatable aspects, was unacceptable. The UGC was of the view that the University College's 'range of activity is too wide in relation to its size'.[7] Again, momentarily, the survival of the University College seemed in the balance. It was 'a contemptuous meeting', as one of the participants, Alwyn Roberts, later recalled,[8] and extensive surgery, subject rationalization within Wales and a sharper focus on the College's strengths were practically demanded of the College.

The revised plan, formulated with the assistance of a 'Special Review Group' chaired by Vice-Principal Geoff Sagar, was ready by the autumn. It signalled a fundamental shake-up of the academic organization. In addition to the Department of Classics and the Italian section of the French and Romance Studies Department ceasing, Physics and Philosophy – departments which, along with Classics, had existed since the College's foundation but which had become small – were to close. There was to be reduced provision in Archaeology. Drama, at least through the medium of English, was destined to be discontinued. Staff in these departments were to be offered early retirement or transfer to other institutions (in fact, a number of transfers were negotiated). Early retirements more generally were also pursued. Other departments were to be amalgamated: Plant Biology, Animal Biology and Biochemistry, for instance, were to form a School of Biological Sciences; Agriculture, Forestry and most of Soil Science became a School of Agricultural and Forest Sciences. In all, with closures and mergers, 26 academic departments were reduced to 16. The academic community well understood the pressures exerted by the UGC, but these developments were taken very much to heart. The Students' Union, too, campaigned against the plan. Amidst considerable emotion (and a student demonstration in support of Philosophy in the Council Chamber during a Senate meeting), the Senate accepted the plan. At the Council, there was an attempt to refer it back, but eventually it was approved by 29 votes to seven.[9]

These had been agonizing decisions for the Principal and his senior colleagues, for they were aware of the impact they would have. Many were utterly downcast. Geoffrey Hunter, Professor of Philosophy, was particularly disconsolate. 'To make the nation leaner, fitter and more competitive in world markets,' he wrote, 'the Department of Philosophy is to be discontinued.'[10] In Arts departments, too, there was deep concern in general, and fury over specific proposals to transfer, along with three staff members, several thousand Classics books to Durham. This led to tense discussion between the two institutions, the Durham Vice-Chancellor acknowledging to his Bangor counterpart that the matter had become 'a problem between us'.[11] Ultimately agreement was reached and a much smaller number of books moved. Nor was indignation confined to staff and students: the distinguished poet, R. S. Thomas, declined the position of Honorary Professor in Bangor in protest against the government cutbacks.[12]

For some, however, there was a sense of relief. Psychology was small and had appeared distinctly vulnerable, but was saved. Chemistry, too, was considered a subject ripe for rationalization in Wales, but at Bangor it was spared. 'The mountain of the University of Wales Rationalisation Committee has strained and brought forth the conclusion that Bangor should be one of the main centres for Chemistry in Wales,' wrote Charles Stirling,[13] Professor of Organic Chemistry who, in 1986, became the sixth Chemistry professor in the College's history to become a Fellow of the Royal Society. Music, too, was considered to have a future in Bangor, though not in Aberystwyth.

The UGC's initial response to the revised plan was broadly favourable, but they were still inclined to press for more. Sir Peter Swinnerton-Dyer, chair of the UGC, wrote supportively by the end of 1986: 'I am sure that a radical approach is right, particularly the proposal to close the Department of Physics.' But he also urged the University College to consider 'whether it has gone far enough'.[14] When a considered response was forthcoming, during a UGC visit to Bangor in November 1987, when implementation of the plan was proceeding, it was declared acceptable by the UGC. Indeed, the Principal and his officers were publicly and heartily commended for their leadership during a difficult period.[15] The Special Review Group, containing the Vice-Principals, together with the Bursar, David Hannah, and the lay chair of the Finance Committee, Wynn Humphrey Davies, was to remain in being to oversee the maintenance of financial discipline. The worst seemed over, although the effects of the restructuring were felt for many years, and bitterness lingered in many quarters. Essentially, four academic departments had closed. Eric Sunderland regretted that it had been necessary, and certainly regretted the strains that it had caused in some relationships. It had been a brutal pruning, but the University College had no choice but to carry it out.

Wrapped in the dark clouds were one or two silver linings. Ocean-ography was set to expand, with the support of the UGC, and seven new appointments were made in 1985/6. The School of Ocean Sciences came into being in August 1986 under the leadership of Denzil Taylor Smith. Economics, led by Alan Winters, had extended its external activities, and had secured sponsorship from a further three major banks by 1986/7. From 1 January 1988, a School of Account-ing, Banking and Economics was formed, essentially recognizing the expansion of their academic interests. External funding was also won by Electronic Engineering (from such schemes as the Engineering and Technology Programme) which enabled some new staff to be appointed. Considerable initiative was shown by Psychology, which deftly negotiated funding from local health authorities for joint university/NHS appointments: some seven such appointments were agreed in 1987/8. Student numbers also began to pick up, having fallen – though not drastically so – in the early 1980s. By 1988/9, they had exceeded 3,300, their highest level so far.

After the shocks and dejection of the early and mid-1980s, the Students' Union began to emerge again as a lively focal point for the social life of students. Its building was renamed 'Steve Biko House' for a period in the late 1980s, and also contained a 'Mandela Bar'. New students found, as one noted, 'a massive range of clubs and societies apart from, I think, hurling . . . and underwater falconry'.[16] The growth of voluntary work by students with the very young, the elderly and the disadvantaged – in 'Community Action' (later renamed 'Student Volunteering') – was an admirable feature which still thrives. From the 1990s, the Summer Ball provided an effervescent end to the academic year, while the development of a night club, Amser/Time, in 1997 proved an ebullient, modern successor to the old Saturday night 'hops'.

The Bangor 'family' had become somewhat extended by the 1990s. With the considerable growth in student numbers, some of the close-knit nature of student relationships, the spirit of warm conviviality, was inevitably lost. The emergence in the 1990s of new self-catering accommodation on the Ffriddoedd site, in place of traditional halls of residence, contributed to a different lifestyle. But this was not an overriding theme. By British and international standards, the University was still not large, and campus life generally retained its homely, small-town feel. Shops and pubs changed identity and new buildings occasionally appeared but the daily stamping ground of students did not change appreciably. It remained true, too, that Bangor graduates formed a more significant proportion of the staff than in most universities. And the family nexus was, in reality, still strong. Even in the twenty-first century, a good few Bangor graduating students could claim that their parents and grandparents were also Bangor graduates.

The national approach to higher education in the 1980s ushered in a period of rapid and fundamental change for universities. The golden age of academic independence and freedom was being displaced by a new, uncomfortable culture based on market values. Performance monitoring, productivity, accountability and value for money became the prevailing dictums. Higher education was to be skewed to be a reflex of economic prosperity and the country's needs. In practice, all university activity and performance was to come under detailed scrutiny. The first Research Assessment Exercise (RAE) – evaluating and grading research performance in each institution – was conducted, albeit in a relatively crude fashion, in 1988. It highlighted excellence in certain specialisms in Bangor, although substantial room for improvement also. The quality of teaching, too, began to be assessed from the 1990s. The University College experienced its first 'inspection' – though it focused mainly on procedures and policies – under the auspices of the new CVCP Academic Audit Unit in 1992 and individual departments and staff were later inspected and judged by the Quality Assurance Agency. Financial probity was also to be more closely checked, and the establishment by the Council of an Audit Committee and of an internal audit function became necessary. The new culture prompted the need for more corporatist or managerial approaches to the running of universities. The Jarratt Report in

1985 recounted what it regarded as numerous management failures in universities and recommended more professional structures, including the formation of planning and resources committees. This duly happened in Bangor, though as in many universities there was a tendency for new structures to be superimposed on the old.

In the late 1980s, a chink of light seemed to offer the University College in Bangor the prospect of a new academic direction. In the aftermath of the cutbacks and departmental closures, there had been a growing sense that it was vitally important for the College to focus on local and regional needs. Building on links developed between the Psychology Department and health authorities, and capitalizing on a national policy to make nursing and midwifery graduate professions (the so-called 'Project 2000' programme), the University College seized on a proposal to absorb the North Wales College of Nursing and Midwifery. Until recently, there had been two separate training schools in Gwynedd and Clwyd (with several hundred students based in Wrexham), but nurse education was undergoing major transformation. After extensive negotiations with government representatives, the health service and professional bodies, agreement was reached. A Faculty of Health Studies, which included a School of Nursing and Midwifery Studies, came into existence in the University College in 1991. Around 80 members of staff formally joined the College, and nearly 700 new students were enrolled on newly validated diploma courses. The erstwhile Principal of the College of Nursing and Midwifery, Philip Pye, became Head of School and Dean of the Faculty. In 1993, Radiography, a much smaller separate college based in Wrexham, also became incorporated as a department within the University College. After a period of retrenchment and difficulty, these were significant developments. Not only was the University College increasing in size, but it was extending its educational reach to encompass a greater element of vocational training and in a way that directly served the north Wales community.

This all seemed in keeping with the drift of public policy. In 1992, in a move at which many in the university sector were aghast, the binary system was swept away by the government and polytechnics also became universities. New funding councils were established, the Higher Education Funding Council for Wales (HEFCW) coming into existence in Cardiff in 1993. Increased and wider participation in university education became a firm policy, although resources remained limited, and it was clear that a funding body dealing with Welsh institutions only would examine more closely than ever the outputs from the Welsh sector.

There were notable developments in other established disciplines. Most striking was the advance of Psychology from a small department which narrowly escaped closure in 1986 to being the largest and most successful department in Bangor. Led by a new head, Fergus Lowe, a child psychologist, a strategy which focused research on three areas (clinical psychology, cognitive neuroscience, and language and learning), extended links with the health sector and recruited staff from across the world, was single-mindedly and triumphantly pursued.

The School of Accounting, Banking and Economics continued to innovate, a new distance-learning MBA programme in conjunction with Manchester University being introduced in 1991. By 1993/4 it had enrolled 600 students in various parts of the world. Significant expertise in optical communications was developed in Electronic Engineering under the leadership of John O'Reilly (later Sir John O'Reilly, Vice-Chancellor of Cranfield University). Sports Science developed as a subject out of the Physical Education division of the School of Education. Its staff displayed considerable research prowess and the School of Sport, Health and Physical Education was established in 1996. (It was renamed Sport, Health and Exercise Sciences in 1999.) Student numbers continued to grow: by 1993/4 there were over 5,000 students at Bangor, and new self-catering halls of residence were built on the Friddoedd site and opened in 1993.

Meanwhile, in 1992, the University College had lost two influential academic leaders all too early. Bedwyr Lewis Jones, a prolific Welsh broadcaster with a popular touch, as well as a respected teacher and researcher, died suddenly at the age of 59. He had led the Welsh Department through stormy times – personally, politically and financially – but his passion for Welsh scholarship, and his deep-seated loyalty to the University College and its roots, never wavered. William Mathias, Professor of Music until 1988 and one of the most prominent modern composers in Britain, died at the age of 58.

In the autumn of 1993, the funding council in Wales was raising the issue of collaboration between the University College and Coleg Normal. Historically, the relationship between the two – though they both trained teachers and their main buildings had been only a hundred yards apart – had been uneven, and occasionally downright suspicious. After the Second World War, a collegiate Faculty of Education, chaired by D. W. T. Jenkins, had been formed to encourage cooperation between the University College, Coleg Normal, St Mary's and Cartrefle College in Wrexham. From the 1950s Coleg Normal had developed specific Welsh-medium teacher training courses, and in the 1970s had diversified by introducing broader arts and social science degrees. The abortive amalgamation attempt in the mid-1970s did not make for the warmest of relationships. By the 1990s, however, they had increasingly common interests, and the whole political and financial environment had changed. The appointment of a new Principal in Coleg Normal in January 1994 represented a crucial step. Gareth Roberts, a mathematician who had spent a year in the University College in 1970/1 as a post-doctoral researcher and had links with the Mathematics Department, came into office anxious to review Coleg Normal's position realistically and to secure a firm future. He consulted widely and quickly judged that he faced problems with the College's estate and substantial financial challenges. Within months, the integration of Coleg Normal with the University College was on the agenda.

In June 1994, the University College Council agreed to initiate discussions with Coleg Normal, and by October the two institutions had agreed a joint statement of intent indicating that they would 'explore expeditiously the principle of integration'.[17] A Joint Working Party, led by Vice-Principal Alwyn Roberts, a skilled negotiator in whom officers and staff of Coleg Normal had considerable confidence, conducted the discussions in a notably positive atmosphere. This was due in part to the fact that leading figures on both sides worked together congenially. They also understood acutely the reality of the situation. Gwilym Humphreys, the chair of the Coleg Normal governors and a prominent advocate over many years of Welsh-medium study, had come to favour integration. Of course there were many issues which required resolution, and assurance which had to be provided. After the University

College Council declared itself willing to proceed with the integration in March 1995 (noting that the Senate was 'in complete agreement'),[18] a series of working groups was established to deal with the practical issues. There were many: academic staff titles, status and grading structures, pensions arrangements and the importance of Welsh-medium provision were among key issues. The name 'Normal' assumed crucial importance, and major debates took place over its possible retention.[19] Each issue was patiently addressed and the way paved for a major development.

Other changes were afoot in the University College. The role and effectiveness of the federal University of Wales were increasingly under the spotlight following the creation of many 'new' universities (including the University of Glamorgan in south Wales). Commissioned reviews – the Daniel Report and the Rosser Report – attempted to strengthen the central features of the federation, but the individual institutions were angling for looser ties. Eric Sunderland took his turn as Vice-Chancellor of the federal University from 1989 to 1991 and found his time and energies spent increasingly on dealing with disagreements and divisions. Consensus did emerge, however, on strengthening the image of the individual institutions. In 1993, Council and Senate in Bangor agreed to change its name to University of Wales, Bangor – the pattern was followed elsewhere in Wales – and in 1994 use of the terms 'Vice-Chancellor' and 'Pro Vice-Chancellor' rather than Principal and Vice-Principal was accepted.[20] The formal legal approval of these adjustments by the Privy Council did not occur until 1997 but, essentially, the title 'University College of North Wales' was no more, and henceforth it would be termed the 'University' and not the 'College'.

While these major breaks with the past were proceeding, Eric Sunderland's Principalship was coming to an end. In December 1993, he announced that he would retire in October 1995. The President, Sir William Mars-Jones, also decided to retire in December 1994, and a group was set up to identify his successor. For Eric Sunderland, it had been an eventful 11 years. His appointment had represented a major turning point for the University College. He had been a warmly engaging Principal with very evident communication skills, but also a tough inner core. Painful decisions had been needed to

address the structural problems of the 1980s, but there was also gratify-
ing development, significant growth and a new mood of optimism.
That the University College survived and was able to build again
was due in substantial measure to his combination of gifts and the
commitment of his senior officers. At his final meeting, the Council
paid tribute to his 'great contribution' since the momentous days of
1984.[21]

The new Vice-Chancellor was Roy Evans. A native of Llandysul in
Ceredigion, and a Swansea graduate, he had spent 26 years in Cardiff
University, including 12 as Professor of Civil and Structural Engineering and four years as Deputy Principal. A Fellow of the Royal Academy
of Engineering, he had won numerous honours in his field, but had
been drawn somewhat reluctantly into administrative affairs in Cardiff.
He had not harboured ambitions to be a Vice-Chancellor. Nevertheless, encouraged by colleagues, he applied for the post of Vice-
Chancellor at Bangor. Sir Charles Evans, as a mountaineer, had been
something of a boyhood hero. And he was aware that there had been
student unrest in the late 1970s, though not perhaps of its deep- seated
nature. Roy Evans deeply impressed the appointment committee and
had already made many friends in Bangor by the time he took up his
post in October 1995.

In June 1995, the new President, too, had been elected. Lord
Cledwyn, a former Anglesey MP and Labour Cabinet Minister, was
a patently wise choice. He was a strong supporter of the University
of Wales and its component institutions; he was highly acceptable to
Coleg Normal staff and governors, and indeed he was a revered figure
in Wales and Westminster.

In significant areas of strategy, the University's course for its next few
years had already been plotted. The integration of Coleg Normal had
been more or less negotiated. (Poignantly, final issues were being resolved as the death of Sir Charles Evans was announced in December
1995.) It duly took effect on 1 August 1996, with the Coleg Normal
Principal, Gareth Roberts, becoming a Pro Vice-Chancellor with specific
responsibility for Welsh-medium activity as well as Head of an enlarged
School of Education. There was also a new School of Community,
Regional and Communication Studies incorporating other Coleg
Normal staff. Importantly, an innovative centre to promote the Welsh

language and Welsh-medium teaching and research – Canolfan Bedwyr – was established.

In 1996, too, the third RAE took place, signalling 'steady progress' in Bangor's ratings and showing that 40 per cent of academic staff were in departments rated 4 or 5, where 5* was the highest rating. Roy Evans had bolder objectives to improve research performance, but would have to wait for five years before a further assessment was to take place. However, he appointed, for the first time, a Pro Vice-Chancellor with specific responsibility for research – Mark Williams, a Professor of Clinical Psychology – and encouraged determined steps to enhance the University's research standing. In the field of teaching and learning, the teaching quality assessment exercise was well under way with half the departments assessed awarded the 'excellent' rating. Courses had been 'modularized' and the academic year semesterized from October 1994, and although this reform had virulent critics, there was to be no going back. To underline his commitment to teaching as well as research, the Vice-Chancellor introduced the notion of 'Teaching Fellowships' – awards which recognized outstanding teaching and student support.

In the area of knowledge transfer (or the 'third mission' as it is sometimes known) Roy Evans fashioned a distinctive approach for Bangor. He was a firm supporter of cooperation with industry and commerce, of applying and – where possible – commercially exploiting knowledge gained during university research. He became an active member of the North Wales Economic Forum, and developed fruitful links with many north Wales businesses. This groundwork made possible the creation of a significant number of Knowledge Transfer Partnerships (originally called Teaching Company Schemes) and strikingly bolstered Bangor's reputation in industrial and business liaison. In 2001, Roy Evans was voted *Daily Post*/WDA Business Person of the Year, and in the following year was appointed CBE.

Student numbers had risen steadily during the 1990s, in part because of the amalgamations in Nursing and Midwifery, Radiography and with Coleg Normal, but in part also because of success in widening access to the University. Bangor was active in the early 1990s in the 'Access Movement' in Wales, and through developing links with further education colleges, the proportion of mature and non-traditional entrants rose from around 12 per cent to approximately 30 per cent in the late 1990s. From 1999, when the Welsh Assembly came into being and began systematically to press for wider participation, the impulse was to sustain this policy. Temperamentally, Roy Evans was a natural collaborator, and he was well placed to pursue the partnership model being promulgated by the Welsh Assembly Government. And it was the University which took important initiatives in this area. Working with the North East Wales Institute (NEWI) and the eight further education colleges in north Wales, a concordat between them was signed in 1998. It was the precursor to the Community University of North Wales Programme, agreed on 2 June 1998[22] and launched publicly in Llandudno in 2000. The 'Community University' was not a 'university' in the traditional sense. It was essentially a framework to facilitate higher education–further education links and student progression, and it helped a significant number of students to move up the qualifications ladder.

By the end of the 1990s, the University had 8,000 students. Its population had doubled within about ten years. Expansion was no longer quite the flashpoint it once was, although its impact was a disagreeable feature to some, especially in the local community. Over 20 per cent of students were Welsh speakers or learners, and Bangor had significantly more studying through the medium of Welsh than any other institution. In 2000, Lord Cledwyn, who was in his 85th year, retired as President. In his five years in office, he had added lustre to the University's activities and was regarded with immense affection. He unveiled a portrait of himself on his last appearance at the University Court in December 2000; sadly, within weeks he had passed away. He was succeeded as President by Lord Elis-Thomas, the first former student and former member of staff to be elected to the position. Dafydd Elis Thomas had graduated in Welsh in the 1960s, and after a brief period as a lecturer in Drama was elected as a member of parliament for Meirionnydd in 1974. He served as President of Plaid Cymru from 1984 to 1991 (during which time he also gained a Ph.D. from Bangor) and he accepted a peerage the following year. By the turn of the century he had become a dignified and respected Presiding Officer in the National Assembly for Wales.

The 'broad mission' – encompassing academic rigour, research excellence, support for business, vocational training and wider access to all courses – recorded achievements. Bangor's challenge, as so often, was its resource base. Whilst student numbers had increased, the recurrent grant from the funding council had not kept pace with inflation. Indeed, reductions in resource – termed 'efficiency gains' – were the order of the day. In particular, the funding settlement for 1997/8 prompted a major new exercise to reduce costs. Savings of £2.5 million per annum were required within two years, and a Restructuring Panel was set up to achieve the necessary economies. The teaching of Russian – which had begun in the early 1960s and had developed under W. Gareth Jones– was discontinued and, importantly, the University Council formally abandoned its long-standing policy of opposition to compulsory redundancies.[23] In the event, a number of posts were lost, but through voluntary means.

By 1999, however, the financial position was again precarious, and more fundamental structural changes appeared the only effective remedy. Again, economies in excess of £2 million were required by 2002/3. The accent this time was to be on a more positive effort to reorganize and strengthen the academic and administrative spheres. A 'Review and Development Panel' set about the painful task of further reducing staffing levels, and major realignments were contemplated. Not all efforts to bring together academic units in seemingly cognate areas were accomplished: Mathematics became incorporated in a School of Informatics, along with Electronic Engineering and an embryonic Computer Science School; but in 2000, a proposal to merge media and communications studies through the medium of Welsh with the Department of Welsh attracted strong opposition and did not proceed.

Even more intractable an issue was the condition of some of the buildings. Many were built before 1940, and even some of those which had emerged from the 1960s expansion were badly in need of repair. The financial constraints since the late 1970s and 1980s had meant a diminishing level of resources being devoted to the upkeep of buildings. As the twenty-first century approached, parts of the estate seemed in terminal decline, and no major capital funding was available from the funding council for general building purposes.

Partnership and cooperation and the sharing of certain services and costs between higher education institutions seemed the only way to free up new resources. It was manifestly the Welsh Assembly Government's policy, set out in *Reaching Higher* in March 2002 following a review. 'Reconfiguration and collaboration' was to be a central plank in the government's platform from that time on. The University in Bangor indicated that it would 'respond positively'.[24] In fact, the University had already moved down this road. In 2001, a 'strategic alliance' had been signed in Ewloe between Bangor and the North East Wales Institute of Higher Education (NEWI) in Wrexham, in the presence of the Minister for Education, Jane Davidson. The value of some level of cooperation between the two institutions had long been recognized. A 'liaison group' had been formed as far back as 1983, and for a brief period 'two plus two' degrees were developed.

In October 2002, a joint paper by Roy Evans, the Vice-Chancellor and Michael Scott, the Principal of NEWI, was placed before the Council. It proposed the examination of two options: a strengthened strategic alliance; and the 'formation of a single university institution in north Wales'. The paper was approved by 18 votes to one.[25] A Joint Project Group was formed, and by March 2003 the Council had agreed to investigate the 'single university' idea in detail. From June 2003, the Joint Project Group was being chaired by Sir Brian Fender, the former chief executive of the Higher Education Funding Council for England.

The 'single university' model – possibly a 'University of North Wales' – had both political and strategic advantages for both institutions. All indications were that it would have secured significant additional funding for higher education in north Wales. From an academic point of view, however, there were complications. For a start, neither Bangor nor NEWI had degree-awarding powers of their own or official university status. Moreover, there was significant distance between the missions and the academic plans of the two institutions, and this, ultimately, was a critical issue. There was one other factor. In the summer of 2003, Roy Evans announced that he would be re-tiring in September 2004. Very shortly after, he underwent major surgery, and was absent from the University. On 5 and 6 December 2003, after 15 months of intensive discussion, the negotiators for the two institutions – without the Vice-Chancellor, who was still recuperating – met in Beaumaris for what was to be the final, crucial discussion. What became apparent was that on the key issues of management and governance of a single university (that is, the processes to appoint a President, a Vice-Chancellor and a Chair of Council), there were markedly different philosophies. When it received a report on 18 December 2003, the Council declared itself 'dismayed' that the size and academic strength of Bangor, in comparison to NEWI, did not seem to be reflected in the composition of the proposed appointment committees.[26] There was a willingness to try to resolve these issues, and some discussion continued, but it was effectively the end of the idea of a 'University of North Wales'. By June 2004, the Council had appointed a new Vice-Chancellor, in succession to Roy Evans, and was preparing to apply for its own degree-awarding powers.

Looking back, Roy Evans believed that the University had been right to explore seriously the possible merger with NEWI; but he also acknowledged that, in the circumstances, the correct decision was eventually taken.[27] There were many other accomplishments during his Vice-Chancellorship. The securing of a new £4 million research vessel for Ocean Sciences in 2001 – a new *Prince Madog* – was a particular source of pride. He had presided over an improvement in research performance – in the 2001 RAE, 77 per cent of staff were judged to be in the top three grades (4, 5 and 5*) – and had made important strides in enhancing the University's contribution to industry and commerce. Building on his old links with Cardiff, and growing activity in the health sphere, he had steered the evolution in 2002 of a 'North Wales Clinical School' in collaboration with Cardiff and NEWI. After several years of hard work and negotiations, a School of Law was established in 2004 – the first major new academic department to be established for over a decade. It had been an arduous furrow to plough: the University had faced increased demands and diminishing levels of resource. But Roy Evans's careful leadership, his modesty and selflessness, his industrious manner and manifest integrity, won admiration in every quarter.

In 2004, for the first time in its history, the University chose an internal candidate and a local man as its Vice-Chancellor – albeit one with wide experience of other universities. Merfyn Jones, Professor of Welsh History since 1994, had been a Pro Vice-Chancellor since 1998 and had served as Acting Vice-Chancellor for three months in 2003 during Roy Evans's absence. In many ways, his career had followed an orthodox path: a native of Meirionnydd, he had graduated from Sussex and Warwick in the late 1960s, had a research post at Swansea and then spent 15 years in Liverpool and had risen to a senior lectureship before transferring to Bangor in 1990 in order to pursue his research in Welsh history. This seemed a highly appropriate move: his first major historical work had been *The North Wales Quarrymen, 1874–1922*. On the other hand, his career had less conventional elements: he had written and presented several historical television programmes, had extensive political contacts and had served as a governor of the BBC since 2003.

In August 2004, Merfyn Jones came into post with an ambitious programme for radical reform. The financial situation, he insisted, was to be turned around (the next four years saw surpluses recorded), and a new drive for academic excellence was initiated. He emphasized research strength as the fundamental basis for advance, but the highest standards were to be sought in every aspect of the University's affairs. Excellence was not an aspiration, he averred, but an imperative. The management and governance structure was thoroughly overhauled, with 80 committees abolished and a greater level of executive decision-making introduced. 'Faculties' were abandoned, and from 2006 academic schools were regrouped into six 'colleges', each of which became a resource centre, aiming, in part, to enable schools to share administrative support and free up academic time for research and teaching. In 2005, the University made a formal application for degree-awarding powers, and after successfully emerging from a ten-month evaluation by the Quality Assurance Agency, the powers and independent university status – with the new title 'Bangor University' – were granted by the Privy Council from 1 September 2007.

Although the University of Wales had at the same time ceased to be a federal organisation, 'reconfiguration and collaboration' between institutions remained the foremost aspect of government policy. A 'research and enterprise partnership' between Bangor and Aberystwyth was agreed in 2006, with the support of £11 million from HEFCW. Finally, a major £70 million redevelopment of the estate was set in train. New en suite, self-catering student accommodation was opened in 2008 and 2009. A £14 million Management Centre (based in refurbished former Coleg Normal buildings) and an imaginatively sustainable 'Environment Centre Wales' building, both opened in 2008 (the latter by Prime Minister Gordon Brown), represented the first steps in the remodelling of the estate. The academic portfolio was also broadening in major ways. The 2008 RAE results showed a notable advance; while in 2001 32 per cent of staff were in units awarded the top two grades, in 2008 47 per cent of research work achieved the highest two ratings (now 3* and 4*). A School of Creative Studies and Media, concentrating on growing expertise in creative industries was launched in 2008. Plans for an exciting 'Arts and Innovation Centre' to replace the Students' Union building and Theatr Gwynedd and to provide modern performance, teaching, support and social facilities were drawn up. Most ambitious of all, plans began to be formulated to develop the study of Medicine in Bangor. All in all, this was a formidable programme of transformation, designed to equip the University to meet the challenges of the future. Meanwhile, Merfyn Jones served a two-year term as Chair of Higher Education Wales (a body representing Welsh higher education institutions) and also a period as Vice-President of Universities UK. In 2008/9, he chaired a major review of higher education in Wales on behalf of the Welsh Assembly Government.

The tempo of change in higher education is unlikely to slow down. The most successful universities in the twenty-first century will be those that possess intrinsic academic strength, but who are also adept at grasping new opportunities and adjusting accordingly. The University in Bangor has travelled far since its early days in the Penrhyn Arms: it has surmounted obstacles, faced crises and, all too often, struggled against the odds. It has also recorded very real academic achievement – much of it unrecognized, and certainly not trumpeted – and has retained a special place in the hearts and minds of many thousands of its students. Even amongst 11,000 students the community spirit and 'family atmosphere' live on. No one can predict the future course with any precision. Doubtless there will be unpredictable challenges, hard choices to make and new academic avenues to explore. What is certain is that the University must never fear change and never compromise on its highest goals; nor must it spurn its great history or its distinctive character.

46. Eric Sunderland,
Principal,1984–1995

47. The centenary: Eric Sunderland (Principal)
and Sir William Mars-Jones (President), lead
the centenary procession from the Penrhyn
Arms portico in October 1984

48. New en suite student residences were opened on the
Ffriddoedd site in 1993

49. Hen Goleg, the original Coleg Normal building, became part of the
University in 1996 and now houses the University's Business School

50. The poet R. S. Thomas accepted his Honorary Professorship in the 1990s, having declined an earlier professorship in the 1980s in protest at government policy

51. Roy Evans,
Vice-Chancellor, 1995–2004

52. Lord Cledwyn of Penrhos
unveils his portrait on his
retirement as President in
December 2000

53. Merfyn Jones, Vice Chancellor since 2004

54. Students volunteering: an arts and crafts session for local children at
Treborth Botanical Gardens

55. The University Chamber Choir, rehearsing with Dame Kiri te Kanawa in 2003

56. Author Philip Pullman, an Honorary Fellow and Honorary Professor in the University, lecturing in the Main Arts Lecture Theatre in 2006

57. Lord Elis-Thomas (President) and the Prince of Wales at the ceremony in June 2007 in Neuadd Prichard-Jones to mark the centenary of the laying of the foundation stone of the Main University Building

58. Prime Minister Gordon Brown, with Vice-Chancellor Merfyn Jones, chats to a student at the opening of the Environment Centre Wales in February 2008

Notes

Chapter 1

1. *Liverpool Mercury*, 20 October 1884, BUA press cuttings.
2. E. L. Ellis, *The University College of Wales, Aberystwyth, 1872–1972* (Cardiff, 1972) [*UCW*], p. 66.
3. J. Gwynn Williams, *The University College of North Wales: Foundations, 1884–1927* (Cardiff, 1985) [*UCNW*], p. 23.
4. Ibid., p. 36.
5. G. Roberts to W. C. Davies, 27 April 1883, BUA.
6. J. Gwynn Williams, *UCNW*, p. 50.
7. Council Minutes, 3 February 1892.
8. Ibid., 5 September 1884.
9. *North Wales Chronicle*, 18 October 1884.
10. Humphreys Owen to Reichel, 10 September 1883, quoted J. Gwynn Williams, *UCNW*, p. 74n.
11. Council Minutes, 27 November 1888.
12. Ibid., 4 March 1889.
13. Ibid., 16 December 1891 and 3 February 1892.
14. Minutes of the Senate Enquiry, 15 November 1892, p. 4.
15. Ibid., p. 41.

[16] Ibid., p. 19.

[17] Ibid., p. 9.

[18] Council Minutes, 21 December 1892.

[19] Ibid., 1 February 1893.

[20] *The Times*, 18 April 1893.

[21] *North Wales Chronicle*, 18 March 1893.

[22] Council Minutes, 11 September 1895.

[23] Quoted J. Gwynn Williams, *UCNW*, p. 114.

Chapter 2

[1] *The University College of North Wales Bangor, 1884–1934* (Bangor, 1934), p. 37.

[2] R. T. Jenkins, 'John Edward Lloyd', DNB, *www.wbo.llgc.org.uk*.

[3] Ibid.

[4] J. Gwynn Williams, *UCNW*, p. 90.

[5] A. R. Owens, 'William Ellis Williams: father of electrical engineering at Bangor' (unpublished paper, 2007), p. 8.

[6] Information supplied by Dr Ll. G. Chambers, 2007.

[7] A. R. Owens, 'W. E. Williams', p. 13.

[8] B. L. Davies, 'The School of Education, UCNW, 1894–1981' (unpublished paper), p. 7.

[9] *Manchester Guardian*, 28 November 1899, BUA press cuttings.

[10] *University College of North Wales, 1884–1934*, p. 11.

[11] *Manchester Guardian*, 14 December 1899, BUA press cuttings.

[12] See J. Gwynn Williams, *UCNW*, pp. 239–50.

[13] *University College of North Wales. Foundation Stone laid by His Majesty the King*, 9 July 1907, p. 11.

[14] *Souvenir of the Opening by King George V*, 14 July 1911, p. 5.

[15] J. Gwynn Williams, *UCNW*, p. 270.

[16] W. Lewis Jones, Introduction, 'Souvenir 1911', p. 3.

[17] Ibid., p. 1.

[18] E. H. Jones to H. Jones, 24 August 1933, BUA.

[19] Lloyd George to Reichel, 3 December 1909, quoted Council Minutes, 15 December 1909.

[20] Information supplied by Professor Martin Taylor, February 2007.

[21] *Welsh Leader*, 11 February 1904.

[22] F. P. Dodd in *The Old Bangorian*, no.6, February 1934, p. 5.

23 J. Gwynn Williams, *The University of Wales 1839–1938* (Cardiff, 1997), p. 116–117.

24 E. L. Ellis, *UCW*, p. 178.

25 Ibid., p. 202.

26 Council Minutes, 21 December 1921.

27 Ibid., 29 September 1919.

28 *University College of North Wales, 1884–1934*, p. 16.

29 *Manchester Guardian*, 28 February 1901, BUA, press cuttings.

30 Council Minutes, 23 April 1924.

Chapter 3

1 Council Minutes, 15 December 1936.

2 J. Gwynn Williams, *UCNW*, p. 438

3 Council Minutes, 27 June 1928.

4 Ibid., 24 April 1929.

5 H. B. Watson, 'Reports of Heads 1929–30', p. 14.

6 R. G. White, ibid.

7 Council Minutes, 9 December 1931.

8 Ibid., 13 December 1933.

9 *Gazette*, vol. 8, no. 1, October 1968, p. 6.

10 P. J. White, 'Reports of Heads 1927/8'.

11 A. H. Dodd to E. H. Jones, 2 September 1933, BUA.

12 J. E. Caerwyn Williams, 'Reports of Heads 1955–56'

13 E. L. Ellis, *UCW*, p. 229.

14 Council Minutes, 26 September 1934.

15 E. H. Jones to M. Davies, 2 December 1936, BUA, Library.

16 G. O. Roberts to E. H. Jones, 24 November 1936, BUA, Societies.

17 S. Griffiths to E. H. Jones, November 1935, BUA, Societies.

18 H. Williams to E. H. Jones, 29 October 1937, BUA, box 42.

19 E. Evans to E. H. Jones, 13 January 1934, BUA, Welsh Studies.

20 UCNW *Calendar*, 1939/40.

21 E. H. Jones to club secretaries, 4 October 1937, BUA, box 42.

22 T. Richards to E. H. Jones, 5 November 1937, BUA, Library and General.

23 E. L. Ellis, *UCW*, p. 253.

24 F. W. R. Brambell, 'Reports of Heads 1935/36'.

25 G. W. Robinson to E. H. Jones, 7 April 1937, BUA, Agricultural Chemistry.

26 D. Thoday to E. H. Jones, 17 May 1939, BUA, Botany.

[27] Council Minutes, 22 June 1938.

[28] J. Gwynn Williams, *The University of Wales, 1839–1939* (Cardiff, 1997), p. 72.

[29] Sir Kenneth Clark to E. H. Jones, 4 September 1939, BUA; notes by National Gallery official, National Gallery Archives.

[30] E. Evans to Sir A. Mawer, 23 May 1939, BUA, box 6.

[31] W. H. Vincent to E. Evans, 28 October 1939, BUA, box 6.

[32] J. W. Fox, 'From Lardner to Massey. A history of physics, space science and astronomy at UCL, 1826–1975', *www.phys.ucl.ac.uk*.

[33] E. Evans to Sir A. Mawer, 10 October 1939, BUA, box 6.

[34] Interview with D. ap Thomas, 12 September 2007.

[35] A. H. Dodd, 'Reports of Heads 1943/4'.

[36] E. H. Jones to E. Evans, 16 October 1940, BUA, Principal.

[37] Council Minutes, 13 December 1939.

[38] Ibid., 25 October 1939.

[39] Ibid., 7 February 1940.

[40] E. H. Jones to M. R. K. Jerram, 26 June 1940, BUA, Forestry general.

[41] H. G. Wright, 'Reports of Heads 1940/1'.

[42] J. L. Simonsen 'Reports of Heads 1941/2'.

[43] J. Morgan Jones, Court Minutes, 24 October 1945.

[44] 'Report of the Council to the Court, 1941/2'.

[45] 'Report by the Post-War Reconstruction Committee, Council Minutes', 27 October 1943.

[46] Reminiscences by Dr Raymond Garlick, August 2007.

Chapter 4

[1] Council Minutes, 26 September 1945.

[2] H. G. Wright, 'Reports of Heads, 1945/6'.

[3] Reminiscences by Dr Raymond Garlick, August 2007.

[4] 'Report of the Council to the Court, 1944/5'.

[5] *Gazette*, vol. 2, no. 1, October 1962.

[6] T. G. Cowling, 'Astronomer by Accident', *Annual Review of Astronomy and Astrophysics*, 1985, vol. 23, pp. 1–19 (6) (online).

[7] J. Ellis Jones, Annual Report, 1988/9.

[8] Council Minutes, 25 September 1946.

[9] E. R. Andrew, 'Reports of Heads, 1955/6'

[10] Acting Registrar to R. S. Thomas, 23 February 1944, BUA, Ballard Matthews.

[11] Reminiscences by Ann Clwyd MP, February 2008.

[12] Reminiscences by Dr Geraint Stanley Jones, October 2007.

[13] *Alpha*, 1948/9, p. 1.

[14] Reminiscences by William G. Smith, 28 August 2007.

[15] 'Report of the Committee appointed by the Senate to consider the problem of extending the use of Welsh', 16 November 1953 (provided by Mr G. B. Owen).

[16] Council Minutes, 27 June 1956.

[17] J. E. Caerwyn Williams, 'Reports of Heads, 1957/8'.

[18] S. Peat, 'Reports of Heads, 1953/4'.

[19] D. Crisp, 'Reports of Heads, 1955/6'.

[20] 'Report of the Council to the Court, 1956/7'.

[21] 'Report of the Council to the Court, 1957/8'.

[22] Interview with Mr G. B. Owen, 5 March 2008.

[23] Interview with Jan Morris, 17 December 2007.

[24] C. Evans to A. McCandless, 6 June 1953, MHT, Charles Evans papers.

[25] C. Evans to A. McCandless, 3 February 1953, MHT, Charles Evans papers.

[26] Jim Perrin, *Spirits of Place* (Llandysul, 1997), p. 103.

[27] Handwritten memoir by Dr Anne McCandless, MHT. Charles Evans Papers.

Chapter 5

[1] Private information.

[2] Jim Perrin, *Spirits of Place* (Llandysul, 1997), p. 101.

[3] Unpublished memoir by Dr Anne McCandless, MHT Sir Charles Evans papers.

[4] 'Report of the Council to the Court', 1958/9 and 1959/60.

[5] C. W. K. Mundle, 'Reports of Heads, 1965/6'.

[6] S. Peat, 'Report of Heads, 1965/6'.

[7] *Annual Report*, 1966/7.

[8] J. M. Thomas, 'Design and chance in my scientific research' in K. D. M. Harris and P. P. Edwards (eds), *Turning Points in Solid State, Materials and Surface Science* (Cambridge, 2008), p.801.

[9] J. L. Harper, *Annual Report*, 1966/7.

[10] Conversation with J. C. Castilla, 15 July 2008.

[11] M. Gavin, *Gazette*, vol. 2, no. 2, January 1963, p. 7.

[12] W. C. Evans, 'Reports of Heads, 1961/2'.

13 R. Poole, 'Memories of John Danby', *Staple*, no. 24, summer 2007. *Staple* is an alumni newsletter produced for English Department graduates.

14 Keith Spalding, *The Long March* (York, 1999).

15 O. E. Evans, *Gazette*, vol. 17, no. 1, October 1977, p. 8.

16 *Gazette*, vol. 14, no. 1, October 1974, p. 9.

17 Reminiscences by Andrew Thomas, 2007.

18 Reminiscences by Mair Barnes, 9 September 2007.

19 Council Minutes, 24 April 1963.

20 Ibid., 9 December 1964.

21 A memorandum to the Petition, November 1962, BUA, Dafydd Glyn Jones papers.

22 C. Evans to D. G. Jones, 6 December 1962, BUA, Dafydd Glyn Jones papers.

23 Council Sub-Committee on the Use of Welsh; document supplied by Mr G. B. Owen.

24 Memorandum to the Council, 'Welsh Language Petition', BUA, Dafydd Glyn Jones papers.

25 Letter to the Council, 13 June 1963; document supplied by Mr G. B. Owen.

26 Council Minutes, 5 February 1964.

27 Ibid., 24 June 1964.

28 *Gazette*, vol. 4, no. 2, January 1965.

29 'Teaching through the medium of Welsh', 24 April 1966; document supplied by Mr G. B. Owen.

30 Interview with Mr G. B. Owen, 5 March 2008.

31 C. W. K. Mundle, *Annual Report*, 1975/6.

32 J. M. Dodd, *Annual Report*, 1970/1.

33 Council Minutes, 27 June 1973.

34 Principal's Report, *Annual Report*, 1975/6.

35 Ibid., 1973/4.

36 'A memorandum to the Court of Governors, UCNW', 1971, BUA, Dafydd Glyn Jones papers.

37 Council Minutes, 27 June 1973.

38 Quoted *Gazette*, vol. 13, no. 2, January 1974, p. 16.

39 Council Minutes, 23 April 1975.

40 Ibid., 25 June 1975.

41 Ibid.

42 Ibid., 4 February 1976.

Chapter 6

1. Council Minutes, 23 June 1976.
2. Ibid., 27 October 1976.
3. O. V. Jones to Lord Kenyon, undated, BUA, Troubles.
4. Bangor AUT Minutes, 23 November 1976, BUA, Troubles.
5. *Caernarfon and Denbigh Herald*, 26 November 1976, p. 10.
6. Sir Thomas Parry to Sir Charles Evans, 16 December 1976, BUA, Troubles.
7. Three students to the Senate, 20 May 1977, BUA, Troubles.
8. Council Minutes, 26 October 1977.
9. Sir Charles Evans to all staff, 16 January 1979, BUA, Bedwyr Lewis Jones papers.
10. Minutes, Non-Professorial Staff Meeting, 26 January 1979, BUA, Bedwyr Lewis Jones papers.
11. Reported in Council Minutes, 7 February 1979.
12. B. L. Jones to Sir Charles Evans, 10 January 1979, BUA, Bedwyr Lewis Jones papers.
13. Students' Union report, *Annual Report 1978/9*, p. 92.
14. Rhys Evans, *Gwynfor Evans: A Portrait of a Patriot* (Ceredigion, 2008), p. 380.
15. Sir Charles Evans to all staff, 16 January 1979, BUA Bedwyr Lewis Jones papers.
16. J. G. Williams to Sir Charles Evans, 20 February 1979, BUA, Bedwyr Lewis Jones papers.
17. B. L. Jones to the Board of Appeal, 7 February 1979, BUA, Bedwyr Lewis Jones papers.
18. Sir Charles Evans to B. L. Jones, 23 April 1979, BUA, Bedwyr Lewis Jones papers.
19. Interview with Professor J. Gwynn Williams, 19 March 2008.
20. J. G. Williams to Council members, 18 April 1979, BUA, Bedwyr Lewis Jones papers.
21. Council Minutes, 25 April 1979.
22. J. G. Williams to C. J. M. Stirling, 10 May 1979, BUA, Bedwyr Lewis Jones papers.
23. Council Minutes, 6 February 1980.
24. J. G. Williams to Lady White, 3 December 1979, BUA, Bedwyr Lewis Jones papers.
25. Principal's report, *Annual Report*, 1978/9, p. 8.
26. Council Minutes, 24 June 1981.

27 Principal's report, *Annual Report*, 1980/1.

28 Signed letter to Lord Kenyon, 13 April 1981, BUA, Bedwyr Lewis Jones papers.

29 Signed statement, 10 April 1981, BUA, Bedwyr Lewis Jones papers.

30 Sir Charles Evans to Anne McCandless, 9 January 1979, MHT, Charles Evans papers.

31 Principal's report, *Annual Report*, 1978/9, p. 3.

32 Council Minutes, 4 February 1981.

33 Aide-memoire for meeting with Lord Kenyon, 8 June 1981, BUA, Bedwyr Lewis Jones papers.

34 Lord Kenyon to Professor W. L. Wilcock, 12 June 1981, Charles Stirling papers (private).

35 Fourteen senior staff to Senate members, 9 June 1981, BUA, Bedwyr Lewis Jones papers.

36 Council Minutes, 24 June 1981.

37 Seventeen staff to Lord Kenyon, 6 August 1981, BUA, Bedwyr Lewis Jones papers.

38 Statement by the Principal, 7 October 1981, BUA, Bedwyr Lewis Jones papers.

39 Information supplied by Professor C. J. M. Stirling, FRS.

40 Council Minutes, 7 October 1981.

41 Sir Charles Evans to Sir Edward Parkes, 3 December 1981, Registrar's Office papers.

42 Ibid., 23 June 1982.

43 Princial's report, *Annual Report*, 1982/3.

44 Council Minutes, 26 May 1983.

45 Sir Charles Evans to Anne McCandless, 5 March 1975, MHT, Charles Evans papers.

46 Council Minutes, 27 June 1983.

Chapter 7

1 Interview with Professor Eric Sunderland, 23 January 2008.

2 Council Minutes, 27 June 1984.

3 R. G. Wyn-Jones, *Annual Report*, 1984/5.

4 Council Minutes, 27 June 1985.

5 Principal's report, *Annual Report*, 1984/85.

6 Council Minutes, 25 June 1986.

7 Ibid., 8 October 1986.
8 Interview with Alwyn Roberts, 20 February 2008.
9 Council Minutes, 8 October 1986.
10 G. B. B. Hunter, *Annual Report*, 1985/6.
11 F. Holliday to E. Sunderland, 4 July 1986, BUA, Dafydd Glyn Jones papers.
12 W. Tydeman, *Annual Report*, 1986/7.
13 C. J. M. Stirling, *Annual Report*, 1986/7.
14 Sir P. Swinnerton-Dyer to E. Sunderland, 7 December 1986, Council Minutes, 4 March 1987, Appendix I.
15 Council Minutes, 2 December 1987.
16 *Seren*, 5 October 1986, p. 2.
17 Council Minutes, 5 October 1994.
18 Ibid., 1 March 1995.
19 Interview with Professor Gareth Roberts, 1 May 2008.
20 Council Minutes, 5 October 1994.
21 Ibid., 28 June 1995.
22 Senate Minutes, 6 July 1998.
23 Council Minutes, 25 June 1997.
24 'Bangor's position in response to the Assembly Strategy', April 2002.
25 Council Minutes, 4 October 2002.
26 Ibid., 18 December 2003.
27 Interview with Professor Roy Evans, 22 February 2008.

Index